WHEN
EAGLES
LAUNCH

WHEN EAGLES LAUNCH

Find Your Best College and Make It a Foundational Life Experience

WILLIAM KEATOR

Surrogate Press®

Published in the United States by
Surrogate Press®
an imprint of Faceted Press®
Park City, Utah

Surrogate Press, LLC
SurrogatePress.com

ISBN: 978-1-947459-32-8
Library of Congress Control Number: 2019917118

Cover design by: Erin Seaward-Hiatt
Interior design by: Katie Mullaly, Surrogate Press®

DEDICATION

For Kelley,
an exceptional wife and mother.

TABLE OF CONTENTS

INTRODUCTION
The Rare Opportunity

When Eagles Launch helps you find more than a college, major, or career. It covers how to find the best college fit—a place where you can excel—*and* helps to prepare for a foundational life experience during your college years. One you can build upon for the rest of your life.

This experience will launch you into adulthood with a base for lifelong education, along with the mental habits and transferable skills you need to succeed personally and professionally. Mental habits, or "habits of mind," control everything you think, say, and do—for better or worse. Transferable skills apply throughout life, no matter the type of jobs, relationships, or situations in which you find yourself.

To hit the ground running in college, think about these questions:

- Can you describe what success will look like in college and in twenty years?
- Do you know deep down what it will take for you—not someone else—to succeed in the way you want?
- Do you really know how college should fit into your life as a whole?

Most students can't provide good answers to these questions, even after college. Yet after reading this book, you should be on your way to having strong answers for these and many more.

College is about *your* life, so you owe it to yourself to dive in and go deep. A surface-level search leads only to a surface-level college fit, and that can easily fall short of what you need to excel.

With college costs having risen steadily for decades, only an exceptional experience, beginning with the right college at the right price, can justify the time and money you will spend. Financial aid does reduce the cost, but aid packages are usually need-based, so college remains relatively expensive for most students—look no further than the $1.5 trillion in loans college graduates still owe.[1]

All of that explains why it's critical to conduct a strong search, and it begins by understanding the rare opportunity college provides.

Each year in the United States, students regularly enroll in two-year or four-year colleges. So it might seem odd for American students to think of college as a rare opportunity, but this changes dramatically when viewed globally. Of the 7.3 billion people in the world, only about 7 percent have earned a college degree or higher.[2][3]

None of this justifies the ever-increasing cost, but college should *never* be taken for granted.

A Wide-Angle View

I began to write this book after working for seventeen years at the Arthur Vining Davis Foundations. If that name sounds familiar, then you probably grew up watching *Arthur, Reading Rainbow,* or other PBS television programs the Foundations have supported for decades.

During this time, I directed two national programs that awarded nearly five hundred grants, totaling over $95 million. The largest

1   Zack Friedman, "Student Loan Debt Statistics In 2019: A $1.5 Trillion Crisis," *Forbes,* February 25, 2019, *https://www.forbes.com/sites/zackfriedman/2019/02/25/student-loan-debt-statistics-2019/#6667e9ad133f.*

2   "U.S. and World Population Clock," United States Census Bureau, July 4, 2018, *http://www.census.gov/popclock/.*

3   "100 People: A World Portrait, 2016," 100people.org, *http://www.100people.org/statistics_detailed_statistics.php.*

of these programs supported private colleges and universities. The other smaller, but still substantial, program awarded funding to new and innovative approaches for the professional development of high school teachers. It also brought me in contact with a number of public universities.

This experience led to a somewhat unique, wide-angle view of higher education. For example, you will see soon why I'm not a fan of college rankings, but if you look at any list of the Top 100 or so liberal arts colleges, I have evaluated and visited most of them at least once—and many more than once.

Equally important for this book, the work included determining which proposals we presented to the Foundations' board of trustees for a final decision. That required my colleagues and me to follow a deliberate decision process.

In the higher education program, we evaluated grant proposals and assessed the overall quality of the colleges and universities seeking support (e.g., academic programs, student activities, student support services, admissions, finances, leadership, etc.). This included campus visits to meet with presidents, administrators, and professors. I also met with students to learn about their experiences, and always asked what they looked for when searching for colleges and why they decided to attend their college.

The First Adult Decision

Some students offered impressive reasons. Yet, too many, even from highly ranked colleges, had shaped their decisions around feelings, assumptions, or faulty perspectives. While most students landed in a good place, many were there for the wrong reasons or for ones that could be classified as surface level.

That's a problem.

These students might have missed the chance to find their best college, and the next time they make a big decision based on poor reasoning, the results could be worse—much worse. Eventually, I realized that where to attend college is (or should be) the first adult decision most students make, so college admissions offers *every* student the benefit of learning how to make an important decision—another opportunity that nobody should take lightly.

Think Differently

This book is different, because it needs to be. Traditional college guidebooks and other online resources help students find a good college, but their approach sticks to a relatively narrow focus. That didn't help the students I met who had struggled with their decisions. And it certainly hasn't curbed the cultural obsession with exclusive, big-name colleges or the heavy debt too many students take on.

More of the same is not the answer.

Instead, everyone involved needs to think a little differently—and more broadly—about colleges, success, decisions, and life. While only a small percentage of students compete for acceptance to big-name colleges and universities, you'll learn in Chapter 1 why the nature of high-stakes admissions can harm more than just those students.

Building Blocks

It's fair to question why I don't focus solely on colleges and universities, especially if you noticed that exclusive college content doesn't begin until Section Four. First, there is college-related material throughout the first three sections. Second, the order in which you think about a decision matters—a lot—and the order of what's covered in this book matters, too.

Skipping around or other shortcuts rarely serve you well. While the final section covers *what you need to do*, the first four sections are building blocks that address *what you need to know* (and why) to maximize your search, college experience, and early adult life.

Section One deals with important big-picture concepts. Section Two tests where you are on making decisions, introduces a number of traps to avoid, and outlines the process you'll be asked to follow. Section Three deals with mental habits and important life lessons that are critical to everything you do. Then, you'll be ready for the college-specific material in Section Four, followed by Section Five, which provides step-by-step guidance on how to make a profession-al-caliber decision on where you go and, equally important, how to prepare for a foundational life experience during college.

Finally, the unusual chapter titles mean we're allowed to have some fun. Let's face it: this subject would be really boring if the book didn't have some quirky parts.

Get Your Head Right

Top performers in any field often talk about the importance of getting their heads right first. In a general sense, that's what a lot of this book is about. You will come to understand:

- Why learning to make big decisions is important *before* you start a college search;
- Why your college experience *must* be viewed in context with life; and
- Why it's important to *dive deeply* into what you pursue.

There are many strong colleges and universities throughout the country, so it's not hard to find a good one, but it can be difficult to find the best ones to meet your personal, professional, and financial needs.

The decisions you make will determine your life's journey. So make no mistake on this: *a college search leads to a big life decision, and the fundamentals for good decision-making will always apply.*

Try, Fail, Reflect, and Correct

To do a proper search, high school students must be deliberate, and that starts by thinking broadly.

When our children began their searches, my wife and I asked them to follow the process you're about to learn. We discussed what would matter the most for them, where they *needed* to go, not where they wanted to go, who they were, and what they valued. We spoke about the importance of making decisions, mental habits, life lessons, and transferable skills.

Finally, we reminded them of the need to *try, fail, reflect,* and *correct*. Get used to these words. You're going to see them a lot and since "failure" is a concept with different meanings for different people, let's go forward with a shared understanding.

Everyone fails throughout life because failure is the most natural path to success. That's why a healthy definition should include everything from falling just short of a goal to total failure—falling flat on your face. The mere thought of complete failure makes people nervous, but these face plants are rare and not worth the nervous energy people devote to them.

To Be Clear

Before starting Chapter 1, I want to be clear on four points:

1. If you're reading this in your senior year of high school, don't worry about coming late to the process. Just get on with it; what we cover will help you catch up.

2. This book is built around your college *search*, which should begin near the end of eleventh grade, while your *path to college* began in ninth grade, choosing classes, extracurricular activities, etc.

3. Some of what's covered might *seem* overwhelming for a high school student, but you can do this. There are chapters with questions and answers at the end of Sections 1–4. Early readers have found these offer helpful clarifications.

4. I'm writing directly to you, and the content revolves around you, but no matter the path, reaching your potential in life includes what you do for others.

This book challenges you to think deeply about college *and* life. By doing that, you can gain a tremendous advantage over the many people who duck the effort it takes to think things through.

FOR PARENTS

A Drama-Free, Healthy Approach

College acceptances are *not* a judgment on your parenting. If there is one, it will occur when your child becomes a parent. Instead, going to college is another life milestone, albeit an important one.

While this book is written to college-bound teens, you are encouraged to read it, especially in today's world where only a rare teenager reads an unassigned, nonfiction book. The contents will help you provide guidance through conversations about college and life—ones that can last well past graduation.

It's Not Too Late

Some of you will consider parts of this book too demanding for a teenager. Obviously, I disagree. Teens are capable of more than many adults might think. While they always need proper support, college-bound teens have the ability for everything this book asks them to do. Of course, whether or not they are willing to do it comes down to the individual.

A few parents might also feel the advice given, mostly in the first three sections, comes too late to help students in the latter stages of high school. That might be true, given the needs of a particular student, but *it's not too late for college*. And if you have younger children, it's never too early to start age-appropriate conversations on many of the topics covered in the early sections.

Avoid Post-College Funk

Since this book is about more than finding a good college, the ideal student outcome will achieve several goals:

1. A drama-free, healthy approach to college admissions, while also learning to make a big decision;

2. A foundational life experience during college; and

3. A strong launch into adulthood.

Combined, these should help avoid "post-college funk"—that all-too-common phase where graduates drift through their twenties, trying to figure out what they want to do in life.

To help their children meet these goals, parents need to step back, guide, and facilitate. Your help will be required, of course, but effective young adults must stand on their own—stripped of Bubble Wrap®—as they try, fail, reflect, and correct, just like we did at the same time in our lives. A student's fears and desires can be obstacles to a quality search/decision, and this can be compounded when parents project *their* fears and desires onto their children.

It's best to let your children think for themselves first, then review their thinking before a final decision is made. If stepping back makes you nervous, a short video featuring Julie Lythcott-Haims, the former Dean of Freshman at Stanford University, should be helpful. You can find this by searching online for "TEDxStanford—Julie Lythcott-Haims—Be Your Authentic Self."

Finally, based on my experience as a parent, teacher, and coach, I think it's safe to say: When you let your children choose their own path, it usually leads back to you.

Fundamentals for College and Life

SECTION ONE

Section One Preview

This section covers important big-picture thinking you must consider before starting a college search and finishes with the introduction of a college-based foundational life experience.

Chapter 1 shows how American culture drives the college admissions frenzy, why true achievement avoids negative influences, and what a college acceptance actually signals.

Chapter 2 untangles commonly held myths about college.

Chapter 3 examines success in school versus success in life and looks at possibilities for defining success.

Chapter 4 highlights fundamentals and why they are taken for granted, despite their critical role in everything we do.

Chapter 5 emphasizes the utmost importance of perspective and the need to develop healthy ones throughout your life.

Chapter 6 introduces three pillars for a foundational life experience during college.

Chapter 7 answers questions you may have up to this point.

Chapter 1

HIGH-STAKES JUMPERS

Cultural Pressure, Achievement, and Acceptance

Nobody lives with a constant awareness of gravity. Likewise, people rarely, if ever, notice how culture shapes their hopes, fears, and decisions—big or small. Cultural pressure pushes broad narratives that try to dictate what you should do, how you should do it, and what you should think.

When you interact with family, friends, and acquaintances, it's nearly impossible to avoid our culture's gravitational pull. Social media, movies, television, and marketing add more pressure. As cultural cues pile up, they can have a positive impact, but they can also limit your potential through groupthink, warped expectations, or needless fears.

Before going further, I want to be clear on this: there is nothing wrong with cultures; however, cultural *influences* can be good or bad, depending on the situation and the needs or abilities of the person they impact.

Peak Insanity

Peak insanity and the cultural avalanche were among my first thoughts when news broke about the FBI's Operation Varsity Blues. That's when we learned about charges against fifty people, including

thirty-three parents, alleging a $25 million bribery scheme for accep-
tances to big-name universities.[1]

Although this level of corruption is an outlier, it was still predictable, due to the long-growing cultural obsession with college
and university reputations. It's a fixation that pollutes college admissions—past and present. And while this scandal is likely to rein in
illegal activity, unhealthy behavior will not go away.

No matter how important it is for students to find their best
college or university—a place where they can excel—the powerful
mix of cultural narratives, competition, and the fear of missing out
will remain, and a number of students (or parents) will always seek
advantages when applying to competitive institutions.

Why?

Go-Go Culture

America probably has the most impatient and competitive culture
in the world. We want results! The American dream is so compelling, we seem wired to want it all and want it now—or be well on
our way to reaching it. Who else would introduce the world to vid-
eo-on-demand, same-day delivery, and matchmaking by swiping
left or right?

American history is filled with accomplishments once thought
to be impossible, and our go-go culture helped drive these. Without
question. But there are negative impacts, too, and one of these—
unhealthy pressure—plays out every day in most American schools,
having long since eroded fundamental values for learning and
development.

1   Devlin Barrett and Matt Zapotosky, "FBI Accuses Wealthy Parents,
Including Celebrities, in College Entrance Bribery Scheme," *Washington Post*, March
12, 2019, *https://www.washingtonpost.com/world/national-security/fbi-accuses-wealthy-
parents-including-celebrities-in-college-entrance-bribery-scheme/2019/03/12/d91c9942-
44d1-11e9-8aab-95b8d80a1e4f_story.html?utm_term=.94c6cdc1ffa4.*

This chapter looks at the major impact American culture has on education, which you need to understand before searching for a college. It follows with an explanation of the key differences between achievement and accomplishment. Too many people misunderstand true achievement. With a better understanding, you can improve your search, college experience, and adult life. The chapter concludes with an explanation of what college acceptances actually signal.

Fictional Extremes

The quickest way to understand how American culture works against educational values is through a brief case study of two fictional extremes—with a twist.

Both extremes track students from their first day of school through high school. But here's the twist: imagine that classrooms and academic subjects are replaced by high jumping. That's it—just teachers, students, a bar, and one of those big mats to land on. Grades are based on getting over the bar with height and style, so I'll refer to the students as jumpers.

The first extreme is an ideal learning environment, while the second extreme injects the same situation with a heavy dose of American culture. Imagine yourself in each one:

- How would you feel?
- What would you do?

Of course, the truth—your truth—lies somewhere in between.

An Ideal Learning Environment

Picture a group of young jumpers on their first day of kindergarten. A few hold back, but most kids are excited and swarm the mat. They launch onto it, over and over again, while their teachers observe, instruct, and encourage. Some kids jump too early, hit the side, and bounce back in a heap. Most land in the middle, bounce up, and smack into each other. Cuts, bumps, and bruises combine with peals of laughter and squeals of delight.

Soon, the children learn to jump without flying off the mat or banging into each other. They do creative, "crazy" jumps with twists and somersaults. Each jumper improves at *their* pace—slowly and steadily for some, quickly for others.

When the bar is introduced, the jumpers can't resist. They have no fear, take turns, and move the bar up or down to a level each jumper wants. They race to the bar, launching over it or into it. Soon the jumpers realize racing doesn't work, so they experiment with different approach speeds and jumping styles. Nobody compares the bar's height or sees missed attempts as failure.

Perfection never occurs to them either, so the jumpers do what kids do: try, fail, reflect, and correct. When jumpers compete, it's healthy, or the kids and teachers work things out.

By high school, the bar keeps rising a little every year, but the jumpers still have passion. They're creative, accomplished, and continue to strive. Late developers—and this is very important—believe it when teachers assure them they will become strong, fast, and agile enough to get over the bar at a high-jump college.

Most jumpers graduate on track to fulfill their potential along with a strong sense of self and achievement.

With American Culture

Let's see what happens with a large dose of go-go culture added to the environment—the chase for the American dream.

The early years are similar. In middle school, some children worry about getting into a good high-jump college, but that comes from their parents. By high school, however, college pressure and anxiety are inescapable. Too many jumpers won't risk their grades, so they only perform jumps they *think* their teachers want to see. It never occurs to them—or their parents—that by narrowing the range of their jumps, they are sacrificing the creativity, experimentation, *and* failure necessary to reach their full potential.

When the media starts to rank high-jump colleges from top to bottom, too many jumpers and parents worry about the future, fear of missing out drives status anxiety, and jumping becomes a high-stakes endeavor. Unhealthy competition, perfectionism, jealousy, and cheating increase, too. (This scenario was written long before the admissions bribery scandal came to light.)

Highly ranked colleges soon become swamped with applications, so they start to look for exceptional characteristics outside of the high-jump pit, which only ramps up stress and anxiety. High-stakes jumpers now sacrifice their summers as unhealthy competition pushes them to build perfect portfolios, overflowing with virtuous activities and accomplishments.

Meanwhile, the many students who can't keep up with the high-stakes jumpers feel unhealthy pressure, too. Many of them lose their sense of achievement, spiral down to just getting by, and fall short of their potential.

Too many jumpers from both groups graduate without a sense of self.

The Cultural Avalanche

Getting into college should be a healthy challenge. Your reality is probably not as extreme as the second example, but our go-go cultural norms still have negative impacts. When the chase for the American dream enters the ideal environment, it pushes an unrealistic narrative, triggers impatience, and allows fear of missing out to take charge.

You know the narrative: all students must excel in school, choose a promising profession as soon as possible, and graduate from a place society considers the best college they can attend. Anyone who strays from this path raises eyebrows. Then, college graduates are supposed to establish an adult life with a great job, great pay, rapid promotions, a nice car, and a perfect house—all of which should be displayed flawlessly through social media.

This is the cultural avalanche, and the avalanche almost always wins. If some readers have their hair on fire with, "But, what if . . ." questions, please be patient. Your concerns will be addressed as the book unfolds.

Draw the Line

Healthy pressure is fine, but unhealthy pressure is toxic. That's where everyone should draw the line. Most students put healthy pressure on themselves naturally, as you saw in the ideal environment.

Think about it.

Humans are born to strive and learn. We figure out how to walk, run, and speak before getting close to a classroom. We're creative and experimental, especially as children and teens. Most of this happens with healthy pressure from within, from being born strivers. Nothing goes off the rails until go-go culture comes into play, and since negative influences aren't going away, all we can do is dodge them, which begins by understanding true achievement.

Box Checkers

Many people might think the high-stakes jumpers are overachievers, but in a real scenario, only a handful would qualify. Jumpers who buy into the high-stakes-whatever-it-takes mindset tend to see their education as a series of boxes to check.

- ☑ Get good grades.
- ☑ Do activities for college applications.
- ☑ Get accepted to a great college.
- ☑ Graduate.
- ☑ Get a high-paying job.

Do you notice the boxes only relate to results? That's the problem.

What too many people see as overachievement is actually rampant box checking. Results matter. Of course they do. *But how you get results and why you want them matters, too.* While the high-stakes jumpers are meant to illustrate an extreme, there are still too many stressed-out students in high schools and colleges across the country.

A big part of that problem comes from their failure to understand how *less can be more.* Box checkers tend to obsess over results. The more results they get, the more boxes they can check, and whoever gets the most checks wins. But if the desired results don't come, their sense of self is at risk. They feel pressure, anxiety, or worse.

That's why a lot of box checkers are less willing to take risks, especially when they think so much is at stake. Some see anything less than perfect as damaging to their self-worth. Never mind that perfection is impossible, and when someone starts down a perfectionist rabbit hole, it's tough to get out.

True Achievement

Achievement is about more than results. True achievement is a healthy pursuit of excellence that should never be confused with perfection or naked résumé building.

True achievers hold interests and find motivation that comes from within. They dive deeply into activities, operating in the healthy middle ground that lies between "good enough" and perfection. Achievers focus deeply on what they do, *not* what they get. For example, achievement-oriented students pursue activities they genuinely want to do, rather than checking boxes for their college applications. They focus on daily excellence, instead of results. And although they worry less about results, they still work hard.

To be fair, box checkers can work hard, too. But their external motivation often ties work to immediate results, so they tend to work just hard enough to get what they want. Meanwhile, real achievers work up to *and* through results. They don't check a box and think "good enough."

Since true achievers accept ups and downs, they're willing to take risks, be creative, and fail. And they keep results in perspective. For example, they understand what a college acceptance actually signals.

What Acceptance Actually Signals

Unhealthy cultural narratives ignore that a college acceptance signals *potential* and *opportunity*, nothing more and nothing less. Admissions committees look for students with the potential to do well, and offer them an opportunity to fulfill their potential.

No matter how low the acceptance rate, there is *no guarantee* students accepted to big-name colleges will maximize their potential. Like every college and university, highly selective ones admit students who thrive, those who manage to get by, and others who struggle for a variety of reasons.

Obviously, acceptance to a college or university with a low acceptance rate is a terrific accomplishment. Of course, it is. But acceptance does not guarantee students have done the work to find a great college fit. It doesn't ensure that students will develop effective mental habits or transferable skills. Nor does it guarantee a high-paying job and a life lived happily ever after.

There are also equally talented students who do not apply to highly selective institutions for many reasons. A number of these students will work hard, maximize their potential, and live fulfilling lives. In five, ten, or twenty years, some of them will equal or surpass some of the students who attended the most highly ranked colleges and universities. There are also late developers who will do the same. You'll see why in Chapter 3.

Everyone Struggles with It

Healthy achievement is not easy. Without realizing it, I was guilty of box checking far more than I want to admit, and you'll struggle with it, too. Everyone does.

Achievement is very important, but 24/7 achievement is impossible. There are times when you have to check boxes. The realistic goal is to know when and why you're doing it.

- Will you go with achievement when it really matters?
- Will you settle for "good enough" or push on for the best result?
- Do you have the courage to do less when others *appear* to be doing more?

Students who strive for achievement are more likely to have a foundational life experience in their college years *and* make better decisions throughout their lives.

Chapter 2

TOASTERS AND HIDDEN GEMS

College Perceptions, Reality, Nonsense, and Value

College admissions is surrounded by misguided thinking that often passes for conventional wisdom. This chapter untangles more of the assumptions built in to the second extreme from the last chapter. In doing so, it debunks three commonly held perceptions about college, explains the fallacy of college rankings, and reveals the irony of highly competitive admissions.

Perception/Reality

Looking past perceptions to uncover reality is an important skill that can improve your search, college experience, and adult life.

PERCEPTION: College admissions is a win-or-lose event. Win through acceptance to a big-name institution, and your life is made. Lose, and your life is over.

REALITY: That's elitist nonsense. Your life's potential is *not* tied to a college's reputation or any admissions decision made at a single point in time. Your college experience will happen in the early stages of what should be a lifetime of learning and development, so there will always be time to reflect, correct, and improve.

The degree to which you learn and develop in college and throughout life—both personally and professionally—is driven by the responsibility you take. *Where you go to college will shape your experience, so that's why it matters, but what you achieve in college and later in life comes down to you—no matter where you go.*

The idea of college admissions as a game has been around for a long time. And if you want to think of it that way, go for it. Play hard. But play the game the right way.

An overarching goal for this book is teaching you how to do that, no matter what others think, say, or do. In short, don't let their problem become your problem.

PERCEPTION: People separate college from life by thinking of it as a bubble. They call it the best four years of their lives, because it's not the "real world." They know college takes work, comes with challenges, and costs money—a lot of money. Yet, the concept of a real world survives. As if there's an on/off switch.

REALITY: You cannot separate college from life. What you do in college and how you do it will be as much a part of life as anything else. Momentum matters, too, because your college years will flow into the "real world," where fictional bubbles burst.

And that's why this book has to be as much about life as it about college.

PERCEPTION: College is a financial transaction. Students invest money for an education, and the credential they earn leads to a higher-paying job and the chance to earn higher-level credentials.

REALITY: This is partially true. Credentials and a higher salary do provide tangible value. No doubt. But thinking that way can lead to a credential-buying mindset that ignores the *full value* of college, which includes intangible benefits that are very hard to pinpoint with a dollar amount.

Your *entire* college experience, including self-discovery, growth, and maturity, will impact how well you launch into adulthood. With extra effort, you can find a great fit at a relatively affordable price.

Viewing college as a financial transaction is understandable, but it begs an important question: Since college costs so much, why focus on just the credential and landing the first job in what might be your first career? Instead, you can think bigger and demand more from your college experience.

College should not be an either-or dilemma where students have to choose between narrow career preparation and a broader preparation for life. You can do both with planning and foresight. The right college will advance you personally and professionally by allowing you to try new things, think new thoughts, and meet new people. The experience will impact the rest of your life, across every aspect of life, and that has tremendous value.

Separating perception from reality never ends. Likewise, how you sort through information to figure out what it tells you and what it doesn't will make a huge difference in your life.

What We Don't See

The result of a college decision is often boiled down to graduation, because that's the big box everyone wants to check. And when high school students head for college, a successful completion is assumed by too many students and parents.

Yet, have you ever wondered how many college students actually graduate or how long it takes them?

The following are graduation rates for public and private four-year colleges and universities across the United States:

Four-Year to Six-Year Graduation Rates for Full-Time College Students[1]

Category	Graduation Rate		
	4-yr.	5-yr.	6-yr
Public colleges/universities	37%	55%	59%
Private nonprofit colleges/universities	54%	64%	66%
Private for-profit colleges/universities	15%	19%	21%

People are often surprised by these percentages, particularly at the *four-year* mark. Feel free to draw your own conclusions on the for-profit colleges/universities.

For our purposes, what the data does *not* show might be more important:

- How many students regretted their decision, but stuck it out anyway?
- How many students thought finding their best college would be easy?
- What percentage never realized they made a flawed decision and how much they missed because of it?

There are many reasons why students fall short of earning a degree, including financial ones. But whether someone graduates or not, I hope these questions help you understand there is more to getting a college decision right than most people realize.

The Fallacy of College Rankings

Let's look at the big perception/reality problem with college rankings. Despite being criticized by serious educators for decades, rankings are an accepted part of American culture. They are often

1   U.S. Department of Education, National Center for Education Statistics, *Digest of Education Statistics 2018*, Table 326.10, accessed October 2019, *https://nces.ed.gov/programs/digest/d18/tables/dt18_326.10.asp.*

used—consciously or unconsciously—when choosing a college or university over another. A lot of the fear-based thinking that drives unhealthy behavior in college admissions can be tied to them, too.

I wasn't kidding about peak insanity and the Varsity Blues scandal. We've probably reached the point where cockroaches and college rankings would be the only survivors of a nuclear meltdown.

Here are some big picture reasons to ignore them.

Institutional Rankings Versus Individual Needs

A credible ranking—one designed for you, me, or anyone else—does not exist. College rankings are based on *institutional* factors, not individual needs. That's why there has never been and never will be a No. 1–best college. If a million students look for a college to meet their needs, there is always a No. 1–best college for each student, and usually more.

Furthermore, most rankings tend to favor colleges and universities that enroll students with the best academic profiles (SAT/ACT scores, grade point averages, etc.), while colleges that enroll students with lesser profiles receive lower ranks, even if some of these colleges do exceptional work with their students.

Think about that.

Students go to college to advance themselves academically, personally, and professionally. Yet, instead of reflecting where students across all levels can find the best place to improve, the rankings are biased heavily toward colleges and universities with the best *entering* students. That's absurd.

- Does the four-year impact on students matter?
- Is it impossible for professors teaching students with average SAT scores to do a better job than professors teaching students with exceptional scores?

- When did a great academic profile become necessary for colleges to maximize a student's potential?

Without credible measurements of the before/after impact colleges have on their students, rankings are just window dressing.

Of course, that's the problem.

An effective evaluation method hasn't been developed. And to be fair, it might be impossible to develop one that accounts for the full range of student needs and performance across the full range of colleges and universities.

Still, none of that excuses the bias institutional criteria have on rankings.

Toasters and Hidden Gems

Generalized rankings also distract from colleges and universities with particularly strong programs, departments, or services, because these peaks of excellence vanish when an entire institution is shrunk to a single number on a long list.

To be clear, *I am not against highly ranked colleges*—only biased rankings. I'm not even against ranking things. If you want to rank toasters, knock yourself out. Just focus on what the toasters eventually produce, not the quality of the bread before a toaster is even turned on.

Do the same when looking at colleges and you'll find there are *many* hidden gems—far more than most people realize—and these institutions are filled with accomplished professionals, too.

That's why my bias is for every student to attend the right college for the right reasons, be it highly ranked or not, public or private, big or small. If a proper search leads to a highly ranked institution, then go for it. Absolutely. However, if you decide to go somewhere because of the reputation, then you've missed the point entirely.

Beyond Face Value and a Rightful Place

Most people who miss on this have a tendency to accept rankings and reputations at face value. Beyond the material covered, I open this chapter with examples of perception and reality to show the importance of finding the truth.

The biggest problem lies with us; we buy into reputations too easily. There's nothing wrong with a fancy label or a great reputation, as long as it's deserved. But at some point, we're all tempted to avoid the work it takes for an informed decision and give in to the comfort a good reputation provides.

That's another reason why it's important you learn to make a big decision. It also explains why a key part of any search is to *confirm* college reputations.

Don't be afraid to ask questions. The best colleges and universities want their reputations tested. That's how they stay ahead. They know entitled thoughts about "a rightful place" at the top will be the exact moment they begin to decline.

The Real Numbers

This leads to the irony of the elite, which is seen clearly by the numbers behind highly selective college admissions. Stick with this. The numbers and percentages make important points. And don't worry, I won't make you roll around with data throughout the book.

In higher education, only so many students can attend the handful of big-name colleges and universities. Since the number of students vying for these spots has grown for decades, acceptance rates have fallen dramatically, which only stresses applicants and fuels the cultural fixation with these institutions.

But is the obsession with big-name colleges and universities justified? Even if the rankings were valid, would acceptance to a highly ranked institution be worth the anxiety and unhealthy behavior this obsession promotes?

To find the answer, I'll use the *U.S. News & World Report* college rankings. These were the first ones to come out in 1983 and are still considered widely to be the most influential. What follows are the top-ranked colleges and universities in the country, according to the *U.S. News* online rankings,[2] along with their first-year enrollment figures, provided by the College Board.[3] Tied scores mean not every rank is assigned, so some are shared. *For our purposes, the combined total of their enrollments is the key number.*

U.S. News & World Report—Top Ten National Universities

Institution by Rank	First-Year Undergraduate Enrollment
1) Princeton University	1,338
2) Harvard University	1,652
3) Columbia University	1,423
3) Massachusetts Inst. of Technology (MIT)	1,114
3) Yale University	1,573
6) Stanford University	1,696
6) University of Chicago	1,809
6) University of Pennsylvania	2,457
9) Northwestern University	1,931
10) Duke University	1,637
10) Johns Hopkins University	1,316
Combined First-Year Undergraduate Enrollments:	**17,946**

---

2   "National University Rankings," *U.S. News & World Report*, 2020, *https://www.usnews.com/best-colleges/rankings/national-universities* and "National Liberal Arts Colleges," 2020 *https://www.usnews.com/best-colleges/rankings/national-liberal-arts-colleges.*

3   College Board's website provides specific information for each institution held in its database. This includes the number of students enrolled in the first-year entering class. The numbers used in this example were sourced from the website in November 2019.

U.S. News & World Report—Top Ten National Liberal Arts Colleges

Institution by Rank	First-Year Enrollment
1) Williams College	533
2) Amherst College	492
3) Swarthmore College	414
3) Wellesley College	614
5) Pomona College	412
6) Bowdoin College	510
7) Carleton College	529
7) Claremont McKenna College	325
7) Middlebury College	628
10) Washington and Lee University	<u>474</u>
Combined First-Year Enrollments:	**4,931**

With little year-to-year movement at the top of the *U.S. News* rankings, these colleges and universities have developed huge brand names and become a gold standard for college admissions.

In a given year about 2.9 million students complete high school, earn a GED, or other equivalent, but, as we see from the combined first-year enrollments, only about 23,000 of these students will enroll in one of the schools listed above.[4] So again, to be clear, these are tremendous institutions where acceptance is a very impressive accomplishment for any high-caliber student.

The Irony of "Elite"

But let's zoom out for a wider perspective—one that includes the 105 colleges and universities assigned a top five through top fifty ranking in the *U.S. News* national categories.

---

4   U.S. Department of Education, National Center for Education Statistics, "Table 302.10 Recent high school completers and their enrollment in college, by sex and level of institution," *https://nces.ed.gov/programs/digest/d18/tables/dt18_302.10. asp.*, accessed November 2019.

These are the institutions where some of the most unhealthy admissions drama can be found. Where, for example, a decline from among the highest ranked of these colleges can be seen as catastrophic when having to "settle" for an institution ranked ten or, even worse, twenty places below. A big reason behind this is that the difference in quality can *appear* to be huge on a list. Except, the actual differences are much smaller. It's also easy to forget there are over four thousand degree-granting institutions in the United States.[5]

As we zoom out, instead of raw numbers, I'll use percentages for the combined enrollments in relation to the 2.9 million students completing high school in a given year.

Percentage of First-Year Students Enrolled in Colleges and Universities with a Top 50 or Above National Ranking from *U.S. News and World Report*[6]

Top 5 — 0.3%

Top 10 — 0.8%

Top 20 — 1.7%

Top 30 — 3.4%

Top 40 — 5.2%

Top 50 — 6.6%

---

5   U.S. Department of Education, National Center for Education Statistics, *Digest of Education Statistics 2018*, Table 317.20, accessed April 2019, *https://nces. ed.gov/programs/digest/d18/tables/dt18_317.20.asp.*

6   The tiers for these percentages are calculated from "National University Rankings 2019," *U.S. News & World Report, https://www.usnews.com/best-colleges/ rankings/national-universities* and "National Liberal Arts Colleges 2019," *https://www. usnews.com/best-colleges/rankings/national-liberal-arts-colleges.* First-year enrollment numbers from the College Board's website, sourced in November 2019, were used to calculate the combined number for each tier. The numerator of 2.9 million high school completers that is used to calculate each percentage comes from the_U.S. Department of Education, National Center for Education Statistics, "Table 302.10 Recent high school completers and their enrollment in college, by sex and level of institution," *https://nces.ed.gov/programs/digest/d18/tables/dt18_302.10.asp.,* accessed November 2019.

While the percentages remain very impressive, this broader look should make it very clear that any angst or unhealthy behavior around admissions is difficult to justify.

Any student who is capable of sending a competitive application to these institutions—from No. 50 to No. 1—is already elite. This caliber of student is highly likely to be accepted somewhere among the elite tiers. Yes, the top fifty is still elite.

I hope you see the irony.

Most of the hype and needless drama around college admissions comes merely from the elite trying to position themselves *within* the elite. That means the students (and/or parents) hung up on the gotta-get-in-or-my-life-is-over mindset are just wasting emotional energy, or worse.

Is the price of unhealthy behavior worth moving up a percentage point or two when a student is already well within or near the *top five percent* of 2.9 million students? No! What about the many hidden gems that still offer terrific opportunities? And yes, if it's the best all-around fit, elite-caliber students can be served well by a hidden gem.

Just In Case

Despite everything I've covered to this point, there will be students (or parents) who still feel the need to go with a college or university that has the best reputation. I've had many conversations with people who are willing to admit that fit matters a lot, but can't let go of reputation "just in case" it turns out to be important. While this can be a relatively harmless reason to buy a lottery ticket, it's a weak excuse for selecting a college.

Instead, finding a college/university where *you* can excel will matter much more to your life's trajectory than generic rankings, warped cultural narratives, or other misguided thinking.

Chapter 3

REMEMBER THE BIRDS AND HORSES

Success in School Versus Success in Life

> "Success is a journey, not a destination. The doing
> is often more important than the outcome."
>
> *Arthur Ashe Jr., the only African-American man to win the singles
> title at Wimbledon, the U.S. Open, and the Australian Open*

M ost students go to college with the ultimate goal of succeeding in life. That's why we need to explore *the idea* of success now.

It's important to think about success in two parts. First, we'll look at the widespread perception that success in school leads to success in life. Then, we'll explore how you can define success. All of this will impact your search, college experience, and beyond.

Success in School Versus Success in Life

The problem when people link "success in school" with "success in life" is that doing so can narrow their definition for success in life. And since the cultural norm for success in school is built largely on grades, students born with brains that are wired for school have a huge advantage. Some even breeze through without much difficulty.

For the remaining students, lower grades might be the best they can do. But if lesser grades represent their best effort, how is that anything less than success? Which leads to two more questions:

- Are students with lesser grades destined to perform at lower levels in life?

- Does the success "A" students have in school guarantee their success in life?

No! And No! Success in school does *not* ensure success in life. It just forecasts further success in school.

While many students do well in school and excel in life, perhaps a major factor for this success comes from their ability to develop strong mental habits and transferable skills while in school and then adapt these to life.

Late Developers

Success in school also favors students who develop on time. Late developers in the classroom are no different than those who are late developing physically. *There is nothing wrong with being a late developer*, and I don't want anyone to read this term with a stigma attached to it.

Maybe late developers need to learn outside of a classroom. After finishing school, some late developers perform to the best of their abilities because now they can focus on one profession (subject), operate in a different environment, or follow a schedule that works better for them.

Even some students who are born wired for school might need time to reach their potential. This explains the late developers who struggle in high school only to thrive in college or graduate school.

All of this highlights why the right fit matters when choosing a college.

A mismatch between your academic profile and a college's profile can result in needless challenges that limit your time for personal and professional development. For example, some students overreach academically, which leads them to struggle in classes, develop poor habits from the need to survive, and miss important opportunities to grow outside of the classroom.

There's a big difference between being challenged and overwhelmed.

Development, Polishing, or Both

You need feedback from teachers and college counselors on your strengths and weaknesses. Try to find a balanced view that doesn't overestimate or underestimate your ability or the type of college you need. Be honest, sometimes brutally honest, when matching your profile to potential colleges.

As a starting point, you can figure out which of the following broad categories best describes you:

- Academic diamonds tend to score high on the SAT/ACT—another element where the right type of mental wiring is a big advantage. They also match their scores with strong grades in challenging high school courses. These students need some academic development, but mostly polishing. (Of course, these diamonds are not guaranteed success in life. They also might enter a college filled with other diamonds. Some will flourish, but others will face classroom adversity for the first time, and 50 percent will be in the bottom half of their class. Depending on their needs, that may or may not be good for them.)

- Late developers fall into a second category. They generally need a more supportive environment than what they have in high school.

- The third category—a mix of the first two—is the largest by far. These students need support in some areas and polishing in others.

Fortunately, there are colleges and universities for each category.

Generally speaking, the so-called elite colleges are designed to complete the development and polishing of academic diamonds, which is easier said than done. There are also colleges and universities that work well with students who have deeper developmental needs, while most institutions are designed to develop or polish students as needed. Yet, the graduation rates you saw in the last chapter show that not all colleges and universities succeed in meeting student needs or students find themselves in the wrong place.

Combining a strong fit with the mental habits covered in Section Three offers the best chance to succeed in college, while a poor fit can lead to problems. Of course, strong habits of mind offer the best chance to overcome a mistake on where you fit.

Let's shift to a broader focus on success in life to see how you might define it.

Defining Success

Culture plays a huge role in how people think about success. For example, Dictionary.com defines success as follows:

"Noun:

1. the favorable or prosperous termination of attempts or endeavors; the accomplishment of one's goals.

2. the attainment of wealth, position, honors, or the like.

3. a performance or achievement that is marked by success, as by the attainment of honors: *The play was an instant success.*

4. a person or thing that has had success, as measured by attainment of goals, wealth, etc.: *She was a great success on the talk show.*

Synonyms: achievement, fame, triumph."[1]

This definition offers an interesting perspective, but you don't have to agree with it.

---

1   Dictionary.com, s.v. "success," updated 2010, *https://www.dictionary.com/browse/success?s=t.*

The Real Secret to Success

Nobody should force a definition of success on you. If you disagree with the definition above, because it includes "wealth, position, honors" and "fame, triumph," feel free to change it. *The real secret to success is that you get to choose, and your definition is the only one that matters.*

Think about that. Then, think about this: "One reason why birds and horses are not unhappy is because they are not trying to impress other birds and horses."[2] Dale Carnegie, once one of the wealthiest and most famous people on the planet, said this. He was right.

Of course, the freedom to define success does *not* mean you should lower goals or settle for less than fulfilling your potential. I've always thought it's best to think of success in big-picture ways. There are certainly goals to set and milestones to reach, but goals/milestones can line up under a big-picture definition, which leaves many ways to define success.

Let's explore a few to help with your definition. We'll look at money and status, happiness and fulfillment, and finish with regrets.

Money and Status

People with unhealthy competitive traits tend to define success too narrowly, especially if they have a results-oriented focus on money, status, or obtaining things. Too often, they *think* this is how they'll find happiness. Money and status can be used as clear goals to aim for on the way to fulfilling your potential, but be careful, because money and status drive a powerful narrative that sucks people in too easily.

If you love the chase, go for it. There's nothing wrong with making money in ethical ways. Just understand that ups and downs will never disappear, and it's pointless to chase big money or status if

2   Goodreads.com, Popular Quotes, s.v. "Dale Carnegie" updated 2018, *https://www.goodreads.com/quotes/22570-one-reason-why-birds-and-horses-are-not-unhappy-is.*

you're miserable doing it. Yes, there are unhappy people with money and status.

Again, don't let their problem become your problem. And always remember: the perfectly curated, ever-so-impressive lives on social media never show the full story of a person's life. *Everyone has issues.* Everyone has high and lows—even those who appear to be the most successful among us. If you come across people (or organizations) that don't think they've got issues to deal with, then that's the first issue they need to address.

Finally, college and making money dovetail for good reasons, but a lot of misguided thinking connects them, which I'll explain when we get to projected earnings in Section Four.

The Journey

This chapter begins with a quotation from Arthur Ashe who was much more than a tennis player. When he broke the color barrier and began winning major tournaments, he used that platform to earn the respect of many people for his views on life.

Ashe's wisdom that "success is a journey, not a destination. The doing is often more important than the outcome" is about *the process*—the day-to-day aspects of doing whatever needs to be done—and reinforces the idea of true achievement outlined in Chapter 1. When players, teams, organizations, etc., focus on daily excellence, good results will follow, because the best process delivers the best long-term results.

If your definition of success revolves around what money and status will bring—the destination—then you risk missing the benefits of getting there—the journey. *Put another way, if you can't be happy on the journey, there's no guarantee you'll be happy at the destination.*

Happiness and Fulfillment

That leads to a definition in which happiness and fulfillment are stand-alone measures for success, one where you strive to reach personal and professional goals by excelling at what you do, because excelling makes you feel good. Deep down, you get the inner satisfaction from overcoming obstacles and pushing past what you had thought were limitations.

In this case, money is secondary to reaching goals. It remains important because everyone has bills to pay, but it's *not* the determining factor for success. Since you'll still reach tangible milestones along the way, money can be a by-product of your broader, more important definition of success.

When pursuing excellence in a profession and your personal life, you're more likely to make enough money, be happy, and live a fulfilling life. Depending on the profession though, you might need to make financial sacrifices that people in other fields don't have to worry about.

You also can't be naïve in choosing a profession. Not many professional basket weavers make it financially, which means certain passions need to be hobbies. Besides, everyone is allowed more than one interest.

Regrets

Another way to view success revolves around regret. Thoughts like, "If only . . ." or "I could have . . ." or "I should have . . ." hold reserved parking places in everyone's mind. A definition for success that limits regret is worth considering.

Balance is important. There will be times when you have to choose between personal and professional goals and commitments. For example, many people sacrifice or delay career ambitions for their family. And if you make a choice like this, you should have realistic expectations for what you can achieve career-wise.

Bronnie Ware is a bestselling author and former palliative care nurse, serving people in the last three to twelve weeks of their lives. Her writing career began after she wrote a simple but powerful online article, "Regrets of the Dying," which lists the top-five regrets she heard from her patients.

What's most striking to me is that her list *excludes* anything related to money or status. Instead, her patients' top regret relates to remorse over a life unlived: "I wish I'd had the courage to live a life true to myself, not the life others expected of me."[3]

Fear and regret tend to go hand in hand. That's why overcoming fear of failure or what others might think is key to minimizing regret.

This brings us back to Ashe, and another piece of wise advice: "You've got to get to the stage in life where going for it is more important than winning or losing."

Live With It

Think carefully about your definition of success. Understand that it will evolve with life experience. Even though it's your definition, other people can serve as role models. Don't change your definition on a whim. Let it evolve slowly. Finally, your definition must be realistic. There's no point in selling yourself short or setting yourself up for failure.

When you have a definition, live with it. Test it during college. Just remember birds and horses are happy because they don't worry about impressing the other birds and horses.

---

3   Bronnie Ware, "Regrets of the Dying," BronnieWare.com, updated 2018, *http://www.bronnieware.com/blog/regrets-of-the-dying.*

Chapter 4

THANK YOU, CAPTAIN OBVIOUS

Fundamentals

> "Learn to do common things uncommonly well;
> we must always keep in mind that anything
> that helps fill the dinner pail is valuable."
>
> *George Washington Carver, American botanist and inventor*

Excellence begins with fundamentals, and it ends without them. The same can be said about a college search and a foundational life experience.

Fundamentals are often neglected, despite being at the core of almost everything people do. The Introduction warned you about shortcuts and how fundamentals for decision making always apply to a college search. Of course, overlooking fundamentals when you're in college or at any point in life will lead to problems, too.

That's why it's so important to understand fundamentals and the reasons people tend to overlook them.

Timeless

How many painters have achieved greatness without mastering brush strokes, or the use of colors, shading, and light? Elite ballerinas can't neglect the basic skills they use in every performance. Where would LeBron James and Steph Curry be without mastering basketball's fundamentals. And even the coolest businesses fail if they're fundamentally flawed.

Fundamentals are also timeless. Think about the quote that began this chapter. George Washington Carver was an African-American born into slavery who still became a significant botanist, researcher, and inventor. What we call fundamentals, Carver called the "common things." What Carver saw as important then remains important today. That will never change.

Two Types of Fundamentals: Skills and Concepts

Fundamentals can be skills or concepts. There are skills people must develop for any activity or profession. Not all skills are basic, but most are recognized easily. Fundamental concepts are just as valuable. They can seem simple, too. For example, Section Two covers how and why a decision is made, yet there is a lot more to these concepts than most people realize.

Ask people what it takes to succeed, and most answers cite fundamental concepts like hard work, making good decisions, and getting along with others. Self-discipline pops up, too. Ask the same question about organizations, and concepts like strategy and workplace culture are added to the mix.

What you rarely hear, though, is someone *identifying* these qualities as fundamentals. Work ethic, discipline, decisions, strategy, and culture are fundamental to success, but they aren't the only ones that fall under this umbrella. While most people point out a few, they miss others, and rarely give credit to the actual umbrella—*the simple idea that fundamentals matter*.

When mistakes happen, people usually point to surface-level problems that are often just symptoms of deeper fundamental flaws. They're skimming rocks on the water, instead of diving in. Yet, nearly every mistake a person or organization makes can be traced back to at least one missing or misunderstood fundamental. This is certainly true for a college search.

Our human tendency to skim leads to an important question: Why do we overlook fundamentals? The short answer is they're too simple, too obvious, and too boring.

Simple

Exceptional people (and organizations) do simple things and understand simple ideas exceptionally well. I want you to remember this, so I'll repeat it: exceptional people do simple things exceptionally well. Unfortunately, simplicity can scare people.

Jack Welch is the legendary former chairman and CEO of General Electric. In a 1989 interview for the *Harvard Business Review*, Welch said, "People must have the self-confidence to be clear, precise, to be sure that every person. . . understands what the business is trying to achieve. But it's not easy. You can't believe how hard it is for people to be simple, how much they fear being simple. They worry that if they're simple, people will think they're simpleminded. In reality, of course, it's just the reverse. Clear, tough-minded people are the most simple."[1]

Please don't confuse simple with *simplistic*. Simple is good, simplistic is not. Simplistic views tend to be rigid and narrow minded. They are often used as weak, feel-good substitutes for concepts that are actually complex. Whereas a simple idea is just simple, and remains open to change, when necessary.

Obvious

Fundamentals are also obvious, which guarantees two problems. First, the insecurity Welch points out about simple things applies to what people see as obvious. How many times have you heard or thought, "Thank you, Captain Obvious"? But just because something seems obvious doesn't mean it's obvious to everyone. And

---

1   Noel Tichy and Ram Charan, "Speed, Simplicity, Self-Confidence: An Interview with Jack Welch," *Harvard Business Review*, September–October, 1989.

even if it is, there's nothing wrong with a reminder. Which brings us to the second problem.

We need to be reminded about fundamentals. Jeff Bezos, Amazon's founder, is quoted widely as saying, "It's very hard to *maintain* a firm grasp of the obvious at all times."[2] While Bezos is talking about business, this concept applies to everything.

Boring

Since fundamentals are simple and obvious, they *will* become boring, and that might be the biggest obstacle to maintaining them. We all want to be interested in what we're doing. But mastering fundamentals takes discipline and repetition. We need to go deeply into whatever we pursue, yet doing the same thing over and over is flat out boring.

We're wide open to fundamentals when we learn something new. We slow down and pay attention to them, until the skill becomes second nature. Then, we get bored and drift away from precision, which is exactly when we cut a finger or trip and fall. These little wake-up calls bring our focus back—until we drift again.

Fundamental ideas get boring, too. They don't sound interesting at lunches, meetings, or conferences. Nor will they yield a bumper crop of "likes" on social media. We know these old ideas are important, yet we still allow *new ideas* to be the shiny objects that catch our eye.

Once this happens, we rationalize anything to trade the simple and obvious stuff for something new and interesting. Or, we look for shortcuts past boring things, like a decision process for a college search. Try to remember that new ideas are flimsy until they're proven, and that always takes time.

2   Todd Bishop, "Jeff Bezos: 7 gems from His Amazon Web Services Talk," Geekwire.com, November 29, 2012, *https://www.geekwire.com/2012/jeff-bezos-5-gems-amazon-web-services-talk/.*

Unlike skills, getting bored with ideas doesn't bring a clear wake-up call. Flawed thinking or flimsy-but-fashionable ideas won't cut your finger or cause an immediate face plant, but the best decision makers ground their thoughts in fundamental ideas and actions.

Embrace It

Don't dismiss something because it seems simple or obvious— embrace it. When problems arise, focus on fundamentals first.

Back to Welch: "Clear, tough-minded people are the most simple."[3] There's no insecurity with people like this. When something is complex, they deal with it. When it's simple, they try not to complicate it. They also *anticipate problems*, so they can be dealt with before becoming more difficult to solve. Finally, they don't get trapped in high-minded attempts to impress themselves or others.

Why?

Excellence begins with fundamentals, and it ends without them.

---

3   *Noel Tichy and Ram Charan,* "Speed, Simplicity, Self-Confidence: An Interview with Jack Welch," *Harvard Business Review*, September–October, 1989.

Chapter 5

DITCH DIGGING

Healthy Perspective Is a Skill

"Some people see the glass half full. Others see it half empty.
I see a glass that's twice as big as it needs to be."

George Carlin, comedian

Perspective—viewing ideas, facts, and life situations in relative importance—is the biggest fundamental anyone can develop. Without perspective, we're lost. And since college admissions is a huge breeding ground for poor perspectives, I need to cover it now, along with the mistaken belief that the right college will *make* you happy.

Perspective will also play a key role during college. Parts of college life will feel like metaphorical ditch digging. There will be times when professors will (or should) give you feedback that's tough to swallow. You might struggle in a few courses or find that others are boring. The same could happen in a summer job or internship.

The perspectives you develop will determine how well you pass these tests and others.

They Doubled Down

In 2003, I visited a highly ranked liberal arts college in New England with a low acceptance rate and an average combined SAT score over 1370. When meeting with the dean of admissions, I was told about a young woman and her father, who were devastated to learn she had been denied.

The father decided to fly from the Midwest to meet with the dean in a hopeless attempt to change an irreversible decision. As the dean put it, they "think her life is over." However, this impressive young woman had been accepted to several very good liberal arts colleges in the Midwest.

While disappointment was understandable, their sense of devastation was not. They had a choice. They could agonize over a single college's denial, which probably would have been a bad fit, hence the decline, or they could celebrate her acceptance to the other colleges.

They *chose* agony.

The father and his daughter had a narrow perspective by believing she had to attend that college to be successful. Then, after her decline, they doubled down on it by reacting emotionally—a weak mental habit—instead of reflecting on her situation to find a healthy perspective.

Your Most Important Skill

Since perspective shapes all of our thoughts, it is a daily challenge that applies to all personal and professional circumstances. Some people might think attitude is more important, but perspective almost always shapes attitude. You are free to choose a point of view for everything you do, see, hear, or read—no matter how major or minor it seems. Even if someone tells you what to think, you're always free to accept or reject it.

Nobody is born with the ability to view themselves, other people, and situations in the most realistic, effective, and healthy ways, and that means everyone can learn how. Don't miss this: finding healthy perspectives is a skill that you can develop.

Google Earth lets you choose how to see its content. Zoom in or out on a fixed point, and the picture changes with the point of view. Zooming applies to life, too. You can learn how to zoom in and out to find the healthiest perspective for *any* life situation, particularly when you face challenges, like being declined by a college, or worse—much worse.

Asking "Why?" is a great way to start. After children learn to speak, they begin to ask, "Why?" That's how they start to make sense of the world and take their first steps on the road to perspective.

Asking "why?" doesn't end with childhood. Adults aiming for healthy perspectives should also ask why-related questions. Why do they feel a certain way? Why do they hold a point of view on something or someone? Is there a better way to think about it?

More specifically, when the father and daughter were devastated by the New England college's rejection, she should have asked:

- Why is it so important to go to that college?
- Why can't I be successful at another college?

Her father should have done the same.

Notice that feel-good descriptions are left out. Positive thinking is important for many life situations, but a healthy perspective doesn't have to be positive or make you feel good. Often, a neutral, realistic point of view is the healthiest. I'll touch on positive thinking in the next section.

The Adult Challenge

Realism should never be confused with negativity. Negative thoughts are a daily challenge for everyone—even the most positive people—and this can be a particular problem in the teenage and early adult years.

Let's put negativity in perspective. Since the world evolves constantly, it brings challenges—big and small—throughout everyone's life. That means feelings are as predictable as the four seasons. Winter breeds uncertainty, a sense of failure, and disappointment, but spring brings renewal through hope, growth, and accomplishment. Fall and summer come, too.

There will always be spring-like ups and winter-like downs. Sometimes you'll see great moments coming, and sometimes you'll be surprised. The same is true for tough times. And all of this applies to everything in life, even the people, places, and situations you love the most.

Effective adults learn how to move past negativity. Anyone can complain and point to what's wrong with life, because the world is massively screwed up in big and small ways. But it's amazing, too. The world is equal parts good and bad, miraculous and tragic. And it always will be.

So the challenge—the adult challenge—is to deal with it in a healthy way.

- Will you jump on negativity, wrap yourself in fear or anger, and shrink from challenges?
- Or will you find perspectives that help you rise up, face challenges, and fulfill your potential?
- What about the groupthink that spreads like wildfire on social media, telling us how to think, act, or feel about something?
- Will you take the easy way and just buy into it?
- Or will you pause, reflect, and develop a healthy perspective, even if yours is different?

How you answer these, through your thoughts and actions, will shape your life.

Perspective Drives Happiness

There are many books written about happiness. I prefer Neil Pasricha's bestselling book *The Happiness Equation*, which offers nine secrets to happiness and ways to lead a more fulfilling life. He had me with the simple and obvious premise: "Be happy first."[1]

For example, if you're going to college, which provides a stunning chance to improve your life, is there any reason not to be happy? But happiness doesn't mean you're always in a blissful state. Happy people have ups and downs, too; they can be frustrated, even downright pissed off, yet for the most part, they consider themselves happy.

Through teaching, coaching, working in the nonprofit sector, and just living life, I've dealt with many people of different ages from all walks of life. Here are some key differences I see between happy and unhappy people: Happy people are engaged and pull themselves out of life's lows. They develop perspectives that bring meaning to their lives and allow them to care more deeply about what they do.

On the other side are unhappy people, not to be confused with those who are temporarily upset. Truly unhappy people tend not to care about much, even to the point where some don't get angry anymore. They're disengaged from their lives, and this usually happens because they struggle with perspective.

These views on happiness do not apply to people who are clinically depressed. Anyone who might be struggling with depression should never hesitate to seek help. There is nothing wrong with reaching out for support.

A College Can't Make You Happy

College should be a happy time in your life. While talking with others about college searches, it was common to hear students (or their parents) say they were looking for a college where they can be happy. Trying to find a "happy place" sounds like a great idea, except there isn't a single college or university that can make you happy.

---

1   Neil Pasricha, *The Happiness Equation* (New York: G.P. Putnam's Sons, 2016), 6.

To understand why, we need to look at happiness and joy, which are often considered the same, but they're not. Joy comes and goes. It's associated with people, situations, and things you do. Happiness, however, is a more permanent, steady state of mind. Joy is feeling good in the moment. Happiness, as you've just seen, survives the times when you're upset. Joy is something that happens, while happiness is a choice.

Although family, friends, activities, and the college you attend can bring moments of great joy, none of these can make you happy. Even going to the college that fits you best will only ensure moments of great joy. As for happiness, that's for you to find, no matter where you go to college and at any point in life.

Happiness comes down to the perspectives you develop, so it's not easy. But you can do it.

There's Ditch Digging and Then There's Ditch Digging

Let's take perspective for a test run using an extreme example that will seem absurd, until it's explained.

Imagine a nice day working at your desk during a summer internship, until the boss hands over a shovel and asks you to go outside and dig a ditch. It needs to be three feet wide, six feet long, and three feet deep. Suddenly, you've got some serious digging to do, even though your internship has nothing to do with ditches.

Since you're a good person and a loyal intern, you dig. You also might have a nasty *inner* monologue or feel sorry for yourself because you got stuck with this absurd request.

But what if you think about it differently?

Maybe the boss is testing you to see if you take pride in your work, no matter how ridiculous it might be. Will you do a half-hearted job or dig the best ditch possible? Or, you could see digging as a Crossfit® workout that allows you to skip the gym and do something else in the evening.

Perspective matters.

Metaphorical ditch digging happens during internships, college, and life. It even happens in dream jobs. CEOs of the biggest companies in the world must still find healthy perspectives daily. Everyone gets stuck doing things they hate and have to find ways to appreciate them.

If you're bored with something, you can zoom in or out to find a perspective that makes it interesting. And don't forget that a healthy perspective matters for every person you encounter.

Always Explain Why

Finally, if you end up being a boss who needs a ditch dug (literal or metaphorical), it's best to explain *why* the ditch is important. For example, the reason behind this chapter's absurd ditch-digging request: "The company is hosting a luau for homeless children, so we need a ditch to roast the pig."

Perspective matters in managing yourself and others. It will matter in your college search and for the rest of your life.

Chapter 6

YOUR MENTAL FREIGHT TRAIN
A Foundational Life Experience

What you find in life mostly depends on what you look for. That's why it's important to understand the components for a foundational life experience *before* you begin a college search.

Three Pillars

A foundational life experience should be built around what *you* need to enter adulthood. I don't believe there is a proven formula or perfect plan, beyond the following pillars:

> Pillar I: Habits of Mind
>
> Pillar II: Education for a Profession *and* Life
>
> Pillar III: Transferable Skills

A well-designed plan that balances each pillar will be your best launching pad into adulthood.

Habits of mind are listed as the first pillar because they drive everything you do. They will impact your education and how well you develop transferable skills.

An *education for a profession and life* goes beyond what you need to know for a career and landing that first job after graduation. The goal should be to establish a base for lifelong learning.

Transferable skills are the skill set you will bring to any job and rely on throughout your personal life. These are critical to your personal and professional development. Some transferable skills overlap with mental habits. Still, I think it's best to separate them. And please don't view transferable skills as less important because they're listed third.

There's a lot more to come on a foundational life experience. For now, it's important to know that *everything* you do during college feeds into a foundational experience, be it classes, student activities, sports, jobs/internships, etc. All of these are vehicles for learning and development.

The Anchor

There is no need for angst if anything seems overwhelming. Books like this present a lot of information at once, which can leave readers with the false sense of a tight timetable. In reality, you'll have time for a proper college search and foundational experience.

The time frame for any goal is critical. Your college should be the best place to anchor *a four- to six-year period* of your life. Don't underestimate the impact of this perspective.

While most students think about "college," you should think of "college years"—a point of view that includes the time before you start and, if necessary, after you graduate. To aim only for what happens on campus is narrow thinking that will limit your overall experience, whereas focusing on the college *years* broadens your view and allows more time for the entire experience—twelve months a year, on- and off-campus.

Don't worry. There's still time for fun and relaxation.

The Real Risk to Future Employment

Students should be open to possibilities when thinking about college. For example, without giving it much thought, many people reject liberal arts majors for career-focused ones (e.g., business, nursing, architecture, etc.). It seems logical because liberal arts majors (English, history, psychology, math, sociology, etc.) don't have straightforward career connections. Yet, they still fit within Pillar II: Education for a Profession *and* Life.

Most people harbor fears that a liberal arts major makes it difficult to land a job. But that distracts from the real risk to future employment, which is *you*. No matter the major or college, you have a personal responsibility to prepare for a career. If you graduate with a liberal arts major and fail to jump on career prep opportunities, then there's no guarantee you wouldn't do the same with a career-focused major, and you would probably need to strengthen some mental habits, too.

Many liberal arts graduates are successful despite the assumed disadvantage of their majors. I'll come back to liberal arts versus career majors in Chapter 22, because every student should consider the difference carefully.

For now, understand that the liberal arts are about fundamentals. These subjects address essential ideas and skills (reading, writing, history, math, and science). The "liberal" in liberal arts has nothing to do with politics. Since this can confuse people, I have long thought the term "liberal arts" should be changed to "fundamental arts" or "foundational arts." And if the word "arts" confuses people, then let's find a different word for that. Whatever it takes to eliminate confusion.

Habits of Mind

Habits of mind are the catalyst for everything you do, including whether or not you pursue career opportunities. They drive *how* you think and *what* you think, but controlling your thoughts is hard. Changing mental habits is no different than a fully-loaded freight train having to slow down, switch direction, and return to full speed.

I will not name and explain easily defined and adopted habits, because life never flows smoothly or fits into those well-designed boxes we use to organize it. Nor is there a simple way to learn effective mental habits. Only deliberate, often messy attempts to develop them will work. I've also found focusing on life lessons from personal experience or those from other people is a great way to start.

You already have a number of strong mental habits. It will take a conscious effort to sustain these, and harder work to improve the weaker ones. You will always need time to try, fail, reflect, and correct. Don't miss reflection. That gets lost or is done too quickly in our high-paced world. Fortunately, the college years offer a safe opportunity to reroute your mental freight train.

Safe? Yes, relatively safe. Would you rather do this during college or after you get a job? Besides, strong mental habits (and transferable skills) will help you get a job *and* excel in it.

A Work in Progress

The most successful people have developed mental habits that propel them to make strong decisions, find healthy perspectives, and reach long-term goals. Their habits of mind also lead to emotional control. They understand mental habits are not something to master. Instead, they are a work in progress for the rest of their lives. So don't mistake the four- to six-year window as an end point for your development.

I hope you notice that I'm highlighting the *most* successful people. There are highly successful professionals who are a mess in their personal lives. Yes, there are trade-offs, but what's the point? The goal should be to balance success *across* your life.

Peaks and Valleys

Effective personal and professional development always depends on a strong understanding of your strengths and weaknesses. Everyone has peaks and valleys. Everyone deals with different circumstances. We can look at averages, but nobody is average across the board.

Anything important in life takes work and you'll need to work on *both* peaks and valleys. If you only work on weaknesses, strengths can decline.

Your profile of strengths and weaknesses (academic, personal, and professional) will be key to finding the best college to anchor a foundational life experience.

Chapter 7

MONSTERS UNDER YOUR BED

Section One Questions & Answers

This chapter addresses questions you might have up to this point.

Do I need my school's college counselor if I read this?

Yes! This book should help you work effectively with a college counselor. The best ones function as life and decision counselors. They deserve more credit than they generally receive, and I have long thought that every school should employ more of them.

With a head start on the thinking I'll ask you to do, a college counselor can spend more time helping find your best options. But if your counselor is overworked, which can happen, this book will help to make up for it.

Do you really expect me to do all this decision stuff?

My expectations don't matter. Only yours do. The goal is a college decision, not a college guess. So how can you make a good decision without knowing how to do it?

Some of the decision-making material in the next section might be intimidating at first glance, especially for high school students. But it's *not* as scary as it may seem. Even adults struggle to make "grown-up" decisions, so imagine the advantage if you can learn to make better ones early in life.

If you feel overwhelmed by anything, understand that we're not talking about a 24/7 grind. You will have to sacrifice time from other activities, but you're going to do that anyway, because setting priorities is part of growing up. A lot of what I'll cover comes down to how you're thinking or what you're thinking about. And since you're going to look for colleges already, this won't add too much time after you've finished the book.

How can I make such a big decision if I'm young and inexperienced?

You have to learn how to make major decisions at some point and where you go to college offers a perfect opportunity. I will always say, "You can do this." But I will *never* say, "You can do this alone."

You'll need a team made up of parents, teachers, coaches, a college counselor, etc. People who know you well and give strong advice.

But if it's a team decision, then it's not really my decision . . .

No. You still have to make the decision, follow through on it, and live with the results. Personal decisions will always come down to you. Yet, good decision makers still get advice from people they trust. Then, they filter it for what they need to hear, not what they want to hear.

Advice is great because you can take it or leave it, *including what's in this book.* But rejecting good advice can be costly. There are times when people hear something that goes against what seems obvious. These head-scratchers are called counterintuitive. You might have read a few already, and there are more to come.

Do mental habits and transferable skills really matter?

Nobody can succeed without good habits and skills—no matter how they define success.

Does a definition of success have to go against culture to be right?

No! But if you go with a cultural narrative, be sure to have strong individual reasons for your definition of success, or anything else.

Why did you write this directly to high school students?

Any students willing to read this deserve to have it written to them.

What if I can only afford a certain type of college?

I'll get to costs later. Until then, the listed cost for a college or university is the "sticker price" and not necessarily your cost. College financial aid reduces cost based on a student's ability to pay, often considerably for students with demonstrated need.

Private colleges generally list higher costs than public institutions, but the privates use an average of 46 percent of their tuition revenue for student financial aid.[1] This tuition discounting means there can be hidden value at private colleges, especially if course availability gets you to graduation in four years, instead of five or more at a public institution—even if the private school costs a little more. Although, in-state tuition costs for public institutions can be difficult for the privates to beat.

---

1   "Private Colleges Now Use Nearly Half of Tuition Revenue for Financial Aid," National Association of College and University Business Officers, May 9, 2019, *https://www.nacubo.org/Press-Releases/2019/Private-Colleges-Now-Use-Nearly-Half-of-Tuition-Revenue-For-Financial-Aid.*

Students who reject possibilities by *assuming* a college will be unaffordable are underthinking their decision. Since financial aid varies from college to college, you can't determine the actual cost until you know the financial aid package from a college that accepts you. There are estimators to help figure out a range when determining where to apply.

What if I just want to find a good college?

There are plenty of good colleges, so it's not hard to find a good one. But the goal should be finding those where you can excel— *the best colleges to meet your personal, professional, and financial needs.* That takes the achievement outlined in Chapter 1, knowing what to look for in colleges and universities, and understanding the decision traps to avoid, which I'll cover in the next section. You can do this, and your team will help.

Why should I bother with this if I already know where I want to go?

Fair question. If you want to go to the University of XYZ, you should still do a proper search. Then, if XYZ remains No. 1:

- You'll learn how to make a big decision;
- If accepted, you'll know beyond any doubt XYZ is the best place for you, along with more good reasons why;
- Your new reasons will also help when the decision is tested; and
- If denied, XYZ was never the best place, but now you have better options.

There are only benefits from exploring possibilities.

What about the technology revolution? What jobs will survive? How much will they change?

That's hard to predict. The coming advances mean everyone should prepare for change, and it's likely to come more rapidly than ever before.

If we look at the past, people have had many jobs throughout their professional lives, and career switches, too. The U.S. Bureau of Labor Statistics found that "Individuals born in the latter years of the baby boom (1957–1964) held an average of 11.9 jobs from age 18 to age 50. . ."[2] Since "half of these jobs were held between the ages of 18 and 24," that leaves an average of six changes from ages 25 to 50.

Looking forward, the hype, doom, and gloom surrounding technology will be impossible to avoid. It's natural to fear *uncertainty*, *change*, and *competition*. Except, these have always been a challenge and always will be, so you can't ignore them or allow them to shape irrational decisions.

Here's the good news.

None of these are monsters under your bed. You can approach them calmly throughout life. Of course, it's difficult when surrounded by dismal predictions.

Are the predictions accurate?

I don't know. There's always hype, doom, and gloom about the future, and advancing technology is no different. Most responsible predictions focus on general outcomes, because it's impossible

---

2   "Number of Jobs Held, Labor Market Activity, and Earnings Growth Among the Youngest Baby Boomers: Results from a Longitudinal Survey Summary," U.S. Department of Labor, Bureau of Labor Statistics, August 24, 2017, https://www.bls.gov/news.release/nlsoy.nr0.htm.

to say specifically what changes will occur and the degree of their impact, but individuals always have different experiences—from great to miserable. So no matter what happens, your specific future—be it good, bad, or in between—is impossible to predict. Although, it's safe to say anyone who ignores the changes to come is likely to have problems.

Okay, so what is generally going to happen?

Here's my opinion. Others will disagree and I could change my mind as events unfold.

Growing advances in technology, including artificial intelligence (AI), means workers are likely to use technology in different ways. People will need to be more agile and adaptable as they develop new skills throughout their professional lives.

Technological advances could certainly allow employers to do more with fewer employees, which means *even the white-collar jobs that many people go to college for could change or be eliminated.* Yet, advancing technology might create new jobs that we can't imagine now. Although, how many jobs is uncertain, too.

A foundational life experience in college should leave you in a better position to deal with change. And while these possibilities can sound scary, always remember that dystopian predictions for an all-is-lost future are just as unlikely to happen as the utopian ones where everyone sings "Kumbaya."

These are the extremes. Reality tends to fall in the middle. We just don't know where. Instead of worrying, track advances in technology while developing your agility and adaptability.

What's not going to change?

Great question! It's equally important to know what will *never* change: the importance of mental habits, fundamentals, life lessons, transferable skills, etc. Artificial intelligence might wipe out smaller, less-important decisions, but big ones might become more important than ever. This will also be true of the need to develop as a person and a professional throughout your life.

Once you acknowledge what will and won't change in the future, preparation becomes a natural part of your life. In other words, if you take care of the future, the future will eventually take care of the present.

Decisions for
College and Life

SECTION TWO

Section Two Preview

This section is relevant to your college search and big decisions for the rest of your life.

Chapter 8 explains the critical role feelings play in decisions and shows the negative impact they had on one young woman's college search.

Chapter 9 covers the importance of *how* you make a decision along with several traps to avoid.

Chapter 10 shows how strong reasons for *why* you make decisions are important before, during, *and* after they are made.

Chapter 11 outlines the interaction between information, beliefs, and interests—the unavoidable factors for any decision.

Chapter 12 illustrates how fear can overwhelm decisions.

Chapter 13 introduces the decision process that shapes a strong college search.

Chapter 14 answers questions that arise from this section.

Chapter 8

THAT WARM-AND-FUZZY FEELING

Wants Versus Needs and a College Experience Gone Wrong

Almost all decisions are riddled with emotion, especially personal ones. This chapter looks at wants and needs, and how emotions can destroy decisions. It ends with the story of how an elite-caliber student's college search led to problems.

Perspective always helps us control and balance emotions, but no part of that means your feelings should be ignored. Instead, the opposite is true: everyone must admit their feelings first to understand and control them.

A Battleground for Wants Versus Needs

Legendary singer James Brown had a hit song that began with "I feel good!" No offense to Mr. Brown, but everyone should avoid what can be called a "James Brown decision." This happens when a person (or group) makes a big decision, gets that warm-and-fuzzy feeling, and thinks, "I feel good!"

Any college search is a battleground for wants versus needs. And since the desire to feel good about big decisions is so strong, it pulls us toward what we *want*—the feel-good no-brainer—rather than what we *need*.

Of course, there is always a time and place for feelings, as long as you limit their influence. Think about the following questions:

- Have you felt overwhelmed by feelings—good or bad—when faced with a decision?

- Has excitement ever led to unrealistic expectations?
- Have you ever wanted a hugs-all-around feeling after you make a decision?

If the answer is yes to any of these, then you know what it's like to lose balance in your thinking.

We also need to eliminate the so-called "no-brainer," which is either an expression for excitement or a weak reason to rationalize what someone wants. So when people think of something as a no-brainer, it usually means their feelings have taken charge of the decision.

Avoid Your Gut

You will feel something immediately about every college you explore, especially during a visit. The issue is when to trust those feelings. The idea of "going with your gut feeling" is just romanticized nonsense people use to avoid the work for a good decision. Anyone who claims to have followed their gut for a good decision was either lucky or put in so much work on the decision their gut feeling was the end result of an informed process.

I've spoken with many students about why they decided on their colleges. The weakest reasons came from students who couldn't get past how they felt. To avoid that, your feel for a place should be used to break ties, after an informed process. For example, a young woman who had been accepted to several strong schools told me she couldn't find an *important* difference among them—a great problem to have. Her trivial tiebreaker was classic: the school where she felt "most comfortable taking a shower."

Let the quality of work you do on a decision shape your feelings.

But in Twenty Years . . .

A college's size, location, vibe, etc., will always tempt you to make a feel-good decision. *But since feelings are fleeting, any decision based on them will fall apart the minute those feelings change.*

Feelings can also distract from asking important questions:

- What will matter the most when you're 40 years old?
- Will the comfort of a smaller campus matter in twenty, ten, or even two years, especially if you need the challenge of a larger environment?
- If you need a small environment, will missing the excitement of a big campus matter later in life?

You need to find the right college for the right reasons—ones that will matter now and later.

A Cautionary Tale

Malcolm Gladwell's bestselling book *David and Goliath* tells the true story of a young woman whom he calls "Caroline Sacks" and how her college experience turned out to be more challenging than expected.[1] As you read this story, pay attention to how Caroline's emotions influenced her decision. Notice how her wants and needs play out. Think about perspective, too, and try to figure out what she missed.

While I want you to focus on Caroline's decision, this story also reveals why academic fit is about more than grades and test scores.

Gladwell describes Caroline as an elite-caliber student who always wanted to become a scientist. She ranked at the top of her high school class, never received less than an A, and crushed her AP tests with "perfect scores." Caroline eliminated one Ivy League university because she "didn't fit the vibe." She also passed on an excellent liberal arts college because it was "fun, but very small."

---

1   Malcolm Gladwell, *David and Goliath* (New York: Little, Brown and Company, 2013), 68–94.

Instead, Caroline chose a different Ivy League university with "a beautiful campus" that had "won her heart." She was accepted and enrolled blissfully, passing on her home state university, which served as her back-up.

Caroline struggled in chemistry during the spring of her first year. She was surprised to find a highly competitive environment. Her fellow students "didn't want to share their study habits." As Caroline put it, "They didn't want to talk about ways to better understand the stuff that we were learning, because that might give me a leg up." She took the same course in her sophomore year and struggled again.

That's when she gave up on a career in science—her lifelong goal.

Relative Deprivation

Gladwell is convinced that if Caroline had gone to her state university, she would be a scientist today. He believes Caroline suffered from "relative deprivation," a term sociologist Samuel Stouffer coined during World War II.

Relative deprivation can have a tremendous influence on what people think, and it starts with poor perspective: the tendency people have to view themselves and their situations only in comparison to the people around them. Instead of zooming out to look at their situations more broadly, people with relative deprivation lose perspective by focusing only on the people around them.

Relative deprivation is a fundamental concept that applies to everything in life. For example, the vast majority of people on Earth are thrilled to just own a car. Yet, those who can only afford an average but still very nice car can feel deprived if they live in a town full of luxury vehicles. That wouldn't happen in a different town, but the sense of deprivation still warps their thinking.

The days are also gone when relative deprivation was a localized issue. Now, social media allows it to go viral. So again, when you see a perfect life on social media, remember that perfection is an illusion. Everyone has issues.

In Caroline's case, relative deprivation hit when she landed in one of the most competitive universities in the country, where students perform at or near the 99th percentile. While Caroline struggled in relation to this group, she might have been a rock star in a class full of 90th- to 95th-percentile students.

Relative deprivation can stir up powerful emotions and cause anyone to lose perspective. In discussing Caroline, Gladwell applies the "big-fish-little-pond" theory, which was developed by psychologist Herbert Marsh.[2] Gladwell sees Caroline as "a little fish in one of the deepest and most competitive ponds in the country, and the experience of comparing herself to all the other brilliant fish shattered her confidence. It made her feel stupid, even though she isn't stupid at all."

Think back to the fictional learning environments in Chapter 1. The second environment saw students spiral down when they compared themselves to the high-stakes jumpers. Like them, Caroline lost perspective, and her sense of self went with it.

As Gladwell puts it, "Students who would be at the top of their class" in a school with more mixed academic profiles "can easily fall to the bottom" in a school filled with exceptional students. And this can lead to "the feeling that they are falling farther and farther behind." Gladwell believes "that feeling—as subjective and ridiculous and irrational as it may be—*matters*. How you feel about your abilities . . . shapes your willingness to tackle challenges and finish difficult tasks. It's a crucial element in your motivation and confidence . . ."[3]

---

2   H. W. Marsh, "The Big-Fish-Little-Pond Effect on Academic Self-Concept," *Journal of Educational Psychology*, 79–3, 1987. *http://dx.doi.org/10.1037/0022-0663.79.3.280.*

3   Malcolm Gladwell, *David and Goliath* (New York: Little, Brown and Company, 2013), 80.

Caroline should *not* have been surprised by the competition at her college. But her search seemed to lack a solid process—one that would have made her acknowledge needs and include them in her search—and that probably sealed her fate. Without a proper structure, emotions controlled her decision.

How different would Caroline's experience and career have been if her college search was about more than a beautiful campus winning her heart? With careful, big-picture thinking about her *needs*, it's likely she would have looked for a more supportive environment. Perhaps, she would have ended up at the "fun, but very small" college and excelled.

When people focus on needs, they usually reach a point where what they need becomes what they want. Always be aware of wants versus needs, control your emotions, and avoid declaring a "dream" college until you reach the end of the process.

Chapter 9

THAT NEW CAR SMELL

How You Make a Decision Avoids Traps

Yogi Berra was a great baseball player for the New York Yankees, who gave us many nonsensical quotes, such as, "When you come to a fork in the road, take it," which allows for an amusing transition into the importance of *how* a decision is made.

The expression "hindsight is 20/20" exists because it's easy to see what should have been done after a mistake. How many times have you heard about a screw up and thought, "What were they thinking?!" But sometimes "*How* were they thinking?" is the better question.

Caroline Sacks' story highlights the importance of having a strong decision process behind your college search. This chapter tests where you are on making decisions and finishes with several traps to avoid.

The following is a quick, fictional case study about a car purchase. Deciding on a college is very different than buying a car, but with either decision, how you make it matters. Try to evaluate what this couple gets right and wrong as they decide on purchasing a car. (The dollar amounts in this example are unrealistic for a young couple, and used only to make clear points.)

The King and Queen of Their Prom

Imagine Brenda and Eddie are the king and queen of their prom.[1] They go to college, land great jobs, get married, and find an inexpensive apartment, which helps them pay off student loans and build their savings to an impressive $50,000. Life is great—until they have to replace their car.

Nostalgic about the old convertible, they still can't wait to smell that new car smell. Brenda and Eddie control their excitement to stay diligent. They see no point in blowing their savings on a fancy $50,000 car. Instead, they have a solid plan to pay $25,000 in cash, keep $10,000 for their emergency fund, and use the remaining $15,000 to start saving for a down payment on a house.

Brenda and Eddie get advice from friends and family. Some tell them they "have to" or they're "crazy not to" buy a certain brand-name car. They know the days of riding around with the car top down and the radio on are over, but they still want a cool car—something that shows how far they've come and how well they're doing. It has to have the right look, be plush on the inside, and include the latest technology.

But they want to have children soon, so whatever they buy must be practical and last for ten years. Eventually, they get over the cool factor by putting possible reactions from friends and family in perspective.

Brenda and Eddie go online to check out options, and weed them down to nine possibilities. Next, they dive into *Consumer Reports* and other ratings to determine the safest, most reliable cars. They also look into the cost for servicing each one over the life of the car.

This research yields five possibilities, which they rank No. 1 through No. 5.

---

1   The inspiration for Brenda and Eddie comes from the Billy Joel song "Scenes from an Italian Restaurant."

On the weekend, Brenda and Eddie visit car dealerships. Option No. 1 is a total bust. What they saw online turned out to be a huge disappointment. Off to the next dealer.

Car No. 2 looks, feels, and drives great. This is the one they want! The car is so perfect they're willing to go a little over budget. Still, Brenda and Eddie drive a hard bargain. They talk the dealer down on the price, negotiate a good trade-in value for their convertible, and write a check for exactly $25,000. They're thrilled to drive away in a new car and start saving for the down payment on a house.

Do Brenda and Eddie make a fundamentally sound decision?

What They Did Right

Here's what they did right:

- They move through the decision process without getting stuck on minor details.
- They use discipline and self-awareness to sort out big-picture needs, move past the cool factor, and negotiate a good price.
- They do homework on safety, reliability, and maintenance.
- Finally, they gain negotiating experience, which will have lasting value when they're ready to buy a house.

This is *very* impressive for a young couple, so it's tempting to grade them with an A or B, but I only give them a C.

Brenda and Eddie make two big fundamental mistakes.

Jumping the Process

There is no need to rank the cars before seeing and test driving all of them first. Doing that causes Brenda and Eddie to lose emotional control and fall into a decision trap that I like to call jumping the process.

The combination of their rankings and knee-jerk excitement for No. 2 make them jump to a conclusion. They drive it, love it, and get so excited that they're probably thinking, "No. 1 stinks, so No. 2 is the new No. 1". But they should question their rankings when No. 1 is a disaster. And without testing all options in their decision pool, how can they know No. 2 is better than the others?

Jumping the process leads to problems. Instead, *trust the process.* If you're caught in a situation where a decision needs to come more quickly than expected, try to accelerate the process rather than jumping ahead. With practice making good decisions, you'll learn to make them more quickly. This is sometimes called "decision velocity."

Fixation

Fixation is another major trap caused by lazy thinking, and Brenda and Eddie fell into it by looking only at new cars. What about used cars? They cut their options in half, or possibly more, when they ignore used cars. What if they could find a similar, low mileage used car for $5,000 to $10,000 less? All they would lose is the new car smell, but that fades away.

Decision Fatigue

While Brenda and Eddie do *not* suffer from decision fatigue, I need to cover the concept. Let's leave the car example and explore this common trap, which usually occurs in two situations:

1. When you're having one of those days (or weeks) that sees decisions pile up—even small ones, such as when to go to the store—you become vulnerable to decision fatigue. If too much comes at you in a short period, it's easy to get worn down mentally and make mistakes. When this happens, it's best to step back, clear your mind, and bring your best thinking to important decisions.

2. Decision fatigue also plays out over time. Let's say a decision doesn't need to be made for three to six months and takes a lot of work. That much time with a decision lurking can wear people down and challenge their patience—even with group decisions. As work and anxiety pile up, the desire to be done with it can be overwhelming, which leads to jumping the process, fixation, or other lazy thinking. Not to mention missing the best decision.

College searches are fertile ground for decision fatigue.

Healthy Versus Unhealthy Bias

Bias is another big decision trap, largely because too many people don't understand the term. In this context, bias refers to people's innate viewpoints, which may or may not be healthy or fair. Since bias often refers to prejudice, most people react negatively to the idea. They want "unbiased" decisions.

Except, unbiased decisions do not exist.

Bias is unavoidable because whatever people want and fear impacts every decision they make. Fortunately, bias can be healthy. When people say they want an "unbiased decision," what they really want is a decision based on healthy or acceptable bias. The challenge is to make decisions with healthy biases instead of unhealthy ones, which begins with healthy perspectives.

Perhaps the greatest challenge to good decision making is *confirmation bias*. This happens when people ignore new information or twist it to confirm what they already want or believe. Everyone is vulnerable to confirmation bias, and I'll dive into that in Chapter 11.

The fundamentals of *how* you make a college decision will matter—a lot. Don't underestimate your ability. You can learn to make great decisions.

Chapter 10

SWIMMING NAKED

Why You Make a Decision Matters—Twice

This chapter covers the importance of developing strong reasons for any decision—ones that hold up over time.

The Human Superpower

"If you don't use your brain, you might as well put it in a glass case and throw sugar at it." Derek Coghlan, an exceptional teacher, said this to my daughter in the eighth grade. He was encouraging her to pursue a challenging path and develop her critical-thinking skills —the ability to analyze information/situations and form a reasoned judgment.

People are born with the ability to think and learn. It's the human superpower. If you want to make great decisions, thinking critically is unavoidable, and the good news is that you don't have to be Einstein to learn how.

Decisions are unavoidable, too. If you run away from them or let others make them for you, you're actually making a decision to avoid decisions. Either way, there will be consequences—good, bad, or indifferent— depending on the situation. And since nobody can escape from thinking or making decisions, the only option is learning to do these well.

Amazon Prime

Let's look at another quick case study. This one revolves around *why* a decision is made. I don't like using money again, because there will be times when it should not dictate your decisions. But numbers can reveal stark differences that make clear points.

Here's a story about Billy Joe and Bobbie Sue, who in this case don't know each other.[1] They each decide to buy Amazon stock and plan to hold their investments for ten or more years, because their research concludes Amazon should become a dominant company. (The following values correspond to Amazon's historical stock prices.)

Magically, Billy Joe and Bobbie Sue buy $1,000 of Amazon stock at the exact same price on July 1, 1999. Their investments climb quickly to $1,700 by November 1. With a big, quick profit to be had, do they take the money and run? Not this time. They feel brilliant, especially when the value keeps climbing.

Then, bang! The stock market crashes. Billy Joe and Bobbie Sue are caught as the historic dot.com bubble bursts. Investors are going nuts, and the I-told-you-so "experts" are having a field day. Billy Joe freaks out, too. He sells his stock for $602 on July 1, 2000. With a big loss, he swears never to do anything so stupid again.

Meanwhile, Bobbie Sue goes back to her original reason for buying the stock. She determines nothing about the business has changed: Amazon should become a dominant company over the next ten to twenty years. She doesn't sell.

But Bobbie Sue is freaking out on October 1, 2001. Her $1,000 investment has dropped to only $140! Meanwhile, Billy Joe doesn't feel so stupid. Bobbie Sue also has a massive case of decision fatigue. She just wants to sell and be done with it. Yet, she sticks to the plan.

---

1   The use of Billy Joe and Bobbie Sue is inspired by the Steve Miller Band's song "Take the Money and Run."

Fast-forward to May 1, 2018. Bobbie Sue was right. Even after another huge plunge during the 2009 financial crisis, her $1,000 investment is now worth a whopping $32,576! And it's still running today. The I-told-you-so crowd is nowhere to be found. As for Billy Joe, he always kicks himself when ordering something on Amazon Prime.

This is an extreme example for illustrative purposes only. *Never invest your savings in only one stock, and consult a professional when you start investing.*

It Will Be Tested

Billy Joe and Bobbie Sue's investments reveal a lot about making decisions. I'll focus on three points:

1. *Do the work to get it right.* Amazon was a great decision. Their research led to the correct reasons why they should buy the stock: Amazon became a dominant company, and its stock price reflected that over time.

2. *Decisions will be tested.* It's naïve to assume a great decision will deliver great results immediately. In this case, Billy Joe and Bobbie Sue had no control over the stock price. Once they bought, their options were limited to selling, holding, or buying more. However, you will need to more actively follow through on most decisions, especially challenging ones like college.

3. *"Why" matters twice.* The reason *why* a decision is made is very important and it remains important. Unfortunately, when decisions are tested, too many people forget why they made them, so when they run into adversity, it's easy to rationalize weak reasons for walking away.

It's okay to bail out of a decision if things change, but that requires strong reasons, too.

Another Partial Truth

Most people would say the *result* of a decision is more important than the reasons for making it. But that's another partial truth. Results obviously matter more for decisions that relate to illness, injury, or life and death. Beyond that, however, *why you do something is more important than any result.*

This can be a head scratcher, so let's dig into it.

Warren Buffett is a world-class investor. One of his most famous lines is, "You only find out who is swimming naked when the tide goes out."[2] This is an amusing way to explain that reasoning is more important than results.

Think about it.

What if a clueless guy makes decisions based on flawed reasoning? In a perfect world, he gets burned, avoids excuses, tries to understand what went wrong, and learns to find better reasons for his future decisions.

Except, the world isn't perfect. So if he continues with flawed logic but his decisions still work out great, then it's okay to think, "This dude's rationale is always screwed up, but the results are great, so whatever." No!

Flawed reasoning *is* flawed. Swimming naked *is* swimming naked, and when the tide finally goes out, you, me, the dude, or anyone else will have a serious problem.

What about the opposite?

You make fundamentally sound decisions based on good reasons, yet your results don't work out. If this keeps happening, should you give up on trying to be a good decision maker, or should you learn to develop better reasons? Which approach leads to the best decisions with the best results over time?

---

2   "Swimming Naked When the Tide Goes Out," *Money*, April 2, 2009, *http:// time.com/money/2792510/swimming-naked-when-the-tide-goes-out/*.

Always remember: The right decisions made for the right reasons will stand up to challenges, and making the right decisions for the wrong reasons will always lead to problems, at some point. *Why* always matters more than the result, except for illness, injury, life, or death.

Unrealistic Positive Thinkers

Many successful people use the power of positive thinking. But I've always thought positive thinkers who succeed are realistic and know how to make good decisions. Since society celebrates success, we don't hear about the positive thinkers who fail. These folks—blinded by their positive but flawed thoughts—don't see trapdoors until they fall through them.

Unrealistic positive thoughts tend to set expectations too high, which can warp your reasoning and lead to poor decisions. Instead, *let the confidence you gain from a good, realistic decision feed your positive thoughts and defeat the anxiety that comes from second-guessing.*

There will be challenges no matter where you go to college, and there might be times when you second-guess your decision. Will you rationalize a reason to transfer, or will you let the strength of why you made the decision help to see it through?

Why matters twice.

Chapter 11

IF IT'S ALIVE, YOU NEVER KNOW WHAT IT WILL DO

Information, Beliefs, and Interests

S tudents often decide to attend the same college for different reasons and there's nothing wrong with that. All decisions (and perspectives) are shaped by a combination of the information we have, our beliefs, and our interests. Together, let's call them our IBI, which are unique and unavoidable.

Chapter 9 covered how bias is inevitable for any decision, and that healthy bias should be a fundamental goal. Your IBI plays a critical role here. This chapter looks generally at each element, explains confirmation bias, which usually involves all three elements, and finishes with the difference between knowledge and wisdom.

Information

Using information correctly allows us to make informed decisions. Fortunately, the information age offers an endless supply. Unfortunately, it comes at us like a fire hose. And there's a ton of garbage mixed in with the good stuff.

Nobody should be naïve. Sorting through the torrent of information taps our critical-thinking skills. It's best to use "book smarts" and "street smarts" to toss the junk and, when necessary, question the motivation behind sources of information.

What you know is important, but *what you don't know* can be even more important, including half-truths or partial information. Ignorance is often mistaken for stupidity, yet ignorance has nothing to do with intelligence. Ignorance means being unaware or lacking knowledge. Depending on circumstances, even the smartest people in the world can be ignorant about things, and when naïveté combines with ignorance, bad things happen.

Brenda and Eddie make two big mistakes, but they're happy because ignorance is bliss. Still, it's not an excuse. Everyone has a personal responsibility to be as informed as possible about the *what*, *why*, and *how* of their decisions. The same is true for groups and organizations.

Beliefs

Beliefs are personal. They shape what you *think* is true and not true, and what you consider important. Beliefs come from information, family, life experience, and culture.

Believing strongly in ideas and values is healthy, if your beliefs don't become set in stone. They can evolve with life experience. In fact, it's already happened. Think back to something you absolutely thought to be true five years ago, but think differently about today.

Even religious beliefs are challenged by life experience, which means some thoughts on faith are likely to evolve. There's nothing wrong with questioning heartfelt beliefs, because doing so may actually strengthen them. You might let some go, tweak others, or reinforce your thinking on those that matter the most.

There are at least two sides to any belief. Remember how running away from a decision is deciding not to make one? Well, choosing to only see one side is choosing ignorance. You don't have to give up views, but it's important to understand why people with different beliefs feel or think the way they do. This helps make better decisions, and people will appreciate that you care enough to understand their beliefs.

One of the ironies of *individual* beliefs is that people seek comfort from others with similar views. It's natural to want personal beliefs confirmed by others, which social media facilitates too easily.

Yet, there are times when big decisions require us to step out of our comfort zone, challenge our beliefs, or stand up to the cultural avalanche—and it might need to happen with your college search.

Finally, some people avoid beliefs. They don't want to be pinned down or dislike passing judgment. But that's still a belief about not having beliefs.

Interests

Interests split into two categories: what is in your self-interest and what you find interesting, rather than boring.

People have a range of interests and abilities, and since we have a natural attraction to things we do well or understand easily, it's natural that our choices and decisions drift in those directions. Darwinism—survival of the fittest—explains why we are wired to sense fear and do what is in our self-interest. At a primal level, we want to survive and care for ourselves.

You should act in your best interest when choosing a college, buying a car, pursuing careers, etc., but self-interest can mess with your mind, because short-term urges cause inner tension. For example, chasing immediate gratification without thinking of what's best in the long term is rarely good for anyone. Yet, short-term urges can still steer people to run with the "cool kids," even when deep down they know it's not the best for the long run.

Finally, people are *not* being selfish when acting in their self-interest. That only happens when self-interest goes too far. You know the type.

Clashing IBIs

Emotions are triggered whenever your information, beliefs, or interests clash. Think about the following questions:

- What happens when new information conflicts with your beliefs?

- What if the information goes against what you think is in your self-interest?

- Or—and this is always tough—what happens if something boring is in your best interest?

Monitor your reactions when something in this book contradicts your beliefs about colleges, success, or making decisions. Do you reject it, or do you slow down and try to understand a different viewpoint? If necessary, do you adjust your thinking?

Confirmation Bias

Mark Twain said, "Get your facts first, and then you can distort them as much as you please."[1] He's taking aim at confirmation bias, which is one of the most common ways people avoid opposing views or uncomfortable situations.

Dr. Shahram Heshmat offers a nice explanation in his *Psychology Today* article "What Is Confirmation Bias?"

> "Confirmation bias occurs from the direct influence of desire on beliefs. When people would like a certain idea/concept to be true, they end up believing it to be true. They are motivated by wishful thinking. This error leads the individual to stop gathering information when the evidence gathered so far confirms the views (prejudices) one would like to be true.

> Once we have formed a view, we embrace information that confirms that view while ignoring, or rejecting, information that casts doubt on it. . . . We pick out those bits of data that make us feel good because they confirm our prejudices. Thus, we may become prisoners of our assumptions."[2]

---

1   Goodreads.com, Popular Quotes, s.v. "Mark Twain," *https://www.goodreads.com/quotes/7041-get-your-facts-first-and-then-you-can-distort-them*.
2   Shahram Heshmat, PhD, "What is Confirmation Bias?" *Psychology Today*, April 23, 2015, *https://www.psychologytoday.com/us/blog/science-choice/201504/what-is-confirmation-bias*.

Any clash within your IBI can trigger fear, insecurity, overconfidence, joy, loneliness, jealousy, love, hate, and more, and those emotions can lead to confirmation bias or other rationalizations that lead to poor decisions.

As my father-in-law likes to say, "If it's alive, you never know what it's going to do." We can add what it will think or say, as well.

Knowledge and Wisdom

Mark Twain also said, "I have never let my schooling interfere with my education,"[3] which leads to the important difference between knowledge and wisdom. Knowledge comes from information, while wisdom is based on knowledge *and* experience. Wisdom is the valuable part of your beliefs that hold up over time.

You aren't too young to possess knowledge, but you're still too young to have wide-ranging wisdom. That's why you need advice throughout your college search from experienced people. Remember, it's a team decision.

College is a tremendous opportunity to build your IBI. No other time in life offers the chance to put such a high concentration on the information you receive, beliefs you form, and interests you explore.

---

3   Matt Seybold, "The Apocryphal Twain: The Study," Center for Mark Twain Studies, November 16, 2017, *http://marktwainstudies.com/the-apocryphal-twain-i-have-never-let-schooling-interfere-with-my-education/*.

Chapter 12

QUICKSAND

Fear and Desire

W e covered the influence emotions and culture have on decisions. Of all emotions, fear is often the biggest obstacle in a college search. This isn't about panic or sheer terror. It's about the fears that lurk in the back of our minds. The ones that can rise up to make even the strongest people rationalize poor decisions. Sometimes people fear failure or what others might think. Some people fear commitment, uncertainty, or change, and almost everyone deals with a degree of self-doubt.

Fears wreak havoc with our decisions *and* our ability to follow through on them. We also tend to project fear onto things—an object or situation—even when doing that is irrational.

Fear and Desire

Fear can also be driven by desire and lead to a circular irony. Ambitious box checkers fall into this trap. It's ironic because a great desire for getting what they want leads to a great fear of missing on what they want so much. They're stuck.

That's why college admissions can be a tremendous battleground for fear and desire, both of which can distract from what you need. *A fundamental challenge for any college search is to overcome fear and control desire.* Only then can you focus on what matters the most—a foundational life experience in your college years.

Spiders and Bees

Deflecting fear is common. A great example comes from a scene in *The Replacements*, a comedic football movie that came out in 2000. The story is based on washed-up replacement players for a professional football league whose regular players have gone on strike. Keanu Reeves starred as the quarterback, while Gene Hackman played the head coach.

How the scene plays out is spot-on for the real world. The coach knows he can only bring out the best in his players if they admit their fears. He begins by saying, "A real man admits his fears. That's what I'm asking you to do. . . ." Obviously, real women do this, too. So we can say mature people admit their fears.

The players respond with banter about minor fears, like spiders. When the coach challenges them, they switch to bees and more banter follows. It's classic deflection, until the coach cuts them off and asks, "Anybody here afraid of anything besides insects?" Silence.

Then the quarterback says, "Quicksand." The players deflect again, jumping on how quicksand literally sucks people in, but the coach cuts this off, too. Then, the quarterback says,

> "You're playing . . . and you think everything is going fine . . . but then one thing goes wrong . . . and then another . . . and another . . . and you try to fight back . . . but the harder you fight, the deeper you sink . . . 'til you can't move . . . you can't breathe . . . because you're in over your head. . . . Like quicksand."[1]

---

1   Deutch, Howard, *The Replacements* (2000; Burbank, CA: Warner Bros).

This quicksand feeling is scary, but it's only a symptom of the real problem—the players' fear of blowing their opportunity at a second chance. Once they admit it, they can deal with it.

Almost everyone deflects at some point and can also relate to the quicksand feeling. It isn't limited to sports and it can easily warp decisions.

Mental Blenders

We all have internal thoughts that bounce around in our heads like a hyperactive three-year-old. Or, you can think of it this way: The human mind is a tangle of wires that powers a big, noisy blender between our ears—all day, every day, at changing speeds. And when fear rises, the blender only takes a nanosecond to hit warp speed.

This inner crosstalk often turns negative because—back to Darwinism—human brains are wired for survival. Without developing an acute sense of fear, our earliest ancestors would've been toast. Refine this sensitivity over the arc of human evolution and the result is us, still searching for danger and reacting with fear.

That's why our thoughts jump on negative information and emotions so quickly. That's also why we are so good at tossing positives into our blenders and turning them into negatives.

Fear, anxiety, and uncertainty always fire up the blender. But let's not be too negative. Excitement fires it up, too. Until we want more. And unless our desires are met, the blender has another reason for a negative wind up.

Finding a healthy point of view is the best way to manage your mind. First, admit that you're wound up. Then, look closely and honestly to determine if the fear that's winding you up is justified. With a little reflection, you will usually find it's just your blender doing its evolutionary job. With that figured out, you can refocus on the fundamentals and anything else that matters. The same is true for great feelings. Enjoy them! Then, put your situation in perspective.

Fear and desire will always be a challenge—before, during, and after college.

Chapter 13

THE PIÑA AND THE COLADA

Three Phases for Your College Search

> "My point is, life is about balance. The good and the bad.
> The highs and the lows. The piña and the colada."[1]
>
> *Ellen DeGeneres, comedian and television host*

With the importance of how and why we make decisions clear, it's time to focus on the structure for making a strong decision. A proper college search is built on a process that provides discipline and develops the durable reasons needed to follow through on it. A strong decision process is like architectural design, so stick to the plan.

Go Big to Middle to Final

There are three phases to a good decision—Big Picture, Middle, and Final—and it's important to follow each one in order.

The Big Picture Phase sorts through your IBI, wants, and needs to determine what matters the most. Since this phase is the farthest from the actual decision, it's the one most tempting to blow off: "Yeah, big picture. I got that."

The Big Picture Phase needs careful thought. It *must come first* because it will frame what you do in the Middle Phase, and these phases combine to frame the Final Phase. Do not take the Big Picture

---

1   Goodreads.com, Popular Quotes, s.v. "Ellen DeGeneres," *https://www.goodreads.com/quotes/498361-my-point-is-life-is-about-balance-the-good-and*

Phase for granted. Quality thought on the front end pays off through a better decision that gets easier to make as the process unfolds.

It's best to approach your college search as follows:

YOUR COLLEGE SEARCH/DECISION PROCESS

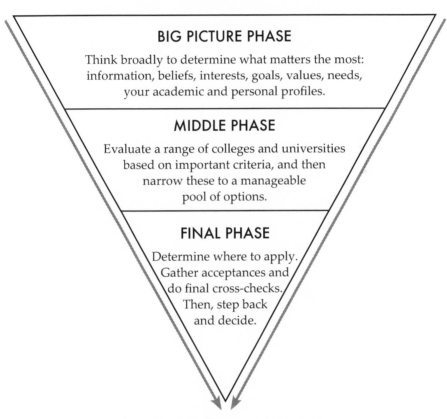

BIG PICTURE PHASE

Think broadly to determine what matters the most: information, beliefs, interests, goals, values, needs, your academic and personal profiles.

MIDDLE PHASE

Evaluate a range of colleges and universities based on important criteria, and then narrow these to a manageable pool of options.

FINAL PHASE

Determine where to apply. Gather acceptances and do final cross-checks. Then, step back and decide.

Your Best College or University

While this process might seem simple and obvious, obstacles always add up to make decisions more challenging than they appear.

The First Mistake

The decision triangle shows the sequence students should follow in a college search. It should also help you understand the first mistake people make: starting in the Middle Phase with early judgments on specific colleges, majors, social life, campus facilities, or other elements. It's a classic example of putting the cart before the horse. If you've already done that, don't worry. Step back. What we cover throughout the book will get you on track.

Think about the inverted triangle. It points to your best decision. But if flawed thinking tilts the Big Picture or Middle Phase in the wrong direction, the result moves away from your best decision, sometimes far away.

Values, needs, and interests matter for any big decision. Without firm thoughts about these first, you can be sucked into either rationalizing what you want or dodging something you fear. This is likely to happen unconsciously, but it still twists big-picture thinking and tilts the triangle toward what you think you want (for example, a big school) instead of what you really need (a smaller, more supportive environment). Or, the opposite could play out—small instead of big.

Yes, decisions can be messed up before they get started. This happens—a lot. Even highly intelligent people fall into this trap, and a college search practically invites it. That's why it's critical to *trust the process,* by following the three phases in order, no matter how tempting a shortcut might seem.

College Visits

College visits early in the Big Picture Phase can be helpful; however, these should aim for gathering information and determining what you need. For some students, visiting different types of nearby colleges and universities allows them to understand and compare what each type has to offer, even if they're unlikely to apply to any of these institutions.

For now, understand that campus visits are about gathering information on where you can have a foundational life experience. Visits are *not* about falling in love with a college because of campus beauty, awesome facilities, or food that's much better than other places. Besides, almost everything on any campus today blows away what previous generations had.

These factors should be used as tiebreakers, when the stuff that matters the most is equal.

Underthinking Versus Overthinking

We've touched on the importance of balance, because it's often overlooked in many aspects of life. Ellen DeGeneres' quotation that begins this chapter gets it right. Life is about balance, and decisions need balance, too. Brenda and Eddie didn't underthink or overthink their car decision.

When hearing about poor college decisions, I can usually put them into three broad categories:

1. *Underthinkers*: This group underthinks college admissions through a laid-back approach that only limits their potential.

2. *Overthinkers*: This group tends to inflate the stakes to the point of hyperventilating over college admissions, but this self-inflicted stress leads to overthinking that clouds their reasoning.

3. *Balanced But Flawed Thinkers*: This group gets the balance right but are caught up too easily in the flawed thinking that passes for conventional wisdom.

The underthinkers need to step it up, while the heavy breathers need to calm down, and the balanced group should think more carefully.

Balance matters in other ways, too. Don't mistake the comments about falling in love with a campus to mean feelings are unimportant. A college search leads to a personal decision that taps your head and your heart. Balancing these will stir positive and negative emotions, so a key goal is to prevent imbalanced reactions that can lead to a poor decision.

Maximizing your college search and decision begins with trusting a well-designed process.

Chapter 14

THAT'S RADIOACTIVE

Section Two Questions & Answers

How do I avoid decision fatigue?

You need to recognize that it's happening. Then, step back to recharge mentally. Walk the dog. Go for a run. Stretch. Meditate. Whatever it takes.

More broadly, trust the decision process, which is how to combat just-get-it-over-with thoughts. And since the process has a finish line, you will learn to pace yourself by knowing what's still to come.

If I end up loving a college my parents hate, what should I do?

A team approach to your decision is likely to prevent that. But if it happens, you'll appreciate the work you put in to make a professional-caliber decision, which is exactly what to rely on in a drama-free conversation with your parents.

Why does it seem like a big decision is actually a lot of small decisions?

I need to define *choices* and *decisions*. Going forward, let's consider decisions to be bigger and less frequent, while choices are smaller, more frequent building blocks toward a final decision.

"If you choose this, then it leads to that" is followed by another "if this, then that." Brenda and Eddie made several choices leading up to their car decision. Likewise, each phase of the decision triangle—Big to Middle to Final—is a broad version of "if this, then that" for the next phase.

All my friends want to go to a certain type of college, but…?

Good friends will support your decision. Great friends will applaud it. Do what's right for you.

Did you go through this process when you were looking at colleges?

No. I wish I had. I went to a good college for the wrong reasons; let's just say I was an early ancestor of the hyperventilation crowd. I pushed myself too hard in high school just to squeak into a competitive college that would quickly reject the same application today. That meant I was burnt out when college started, which can happen. I also fell hard for that college-is-not-the-real-world garbage.

The combination of being a knucklehead, burnout, and essentially majoring in rebellion meant I was *never* going to fulfill my potential in college. Did I learn anything? Yes, but that's a credit to the college, not me. And I didn't learn as much as I could have, so I wasted a great opportunity.

When we became parents, my wife and I wanted our children to avoid these problems and others. Apparently, it worked. They've urged me to write this book for years so other students can learn what they came to think of as a low-pressure process.

There's more to come on work and pressure. For now, don't mistake low-pressure to mean less work.

It's obvious how negative emotions can mess up a decision, but why should I keep positive emotions in check?

Excitement caused Brenda and Eddie to jump the process, and Caroline Sacks was caught up in positive feelings, too. Still, I want to be very clear on this. Always savor good feelings. Take time to laugh, smile, and enjoy the satisfaction of a job well done. Then, tap the brakes. Zoom out to look at your situation calmly, clearly, and realistically.

Positive feelings can also distract from fundamentals. When people are excited, they can overestimate their abilities and set their expectations too high—or they take fundamentals for granted. Good feelings can also suck people into doing too much, too fast, and burning out.

Almost any situation is never as good or bad as it seems.

What about high school relationships? Should I pick a college close to my significant other?

That's a radioactive question. I shouldn't touch this, but...you should do a search to find *your* best college. If that means distance on a high school relationship, then so be it. If either of you go where you don't fit, it could strain the relationship. Besides, a strong one can survive distance.

Of course, this is just my opinion.

Are you going to recommend a list of colleges and universities?

No. First, this book is built on what you need to know and think about *before* you start a college search. Second, it's written for a broad audience. A list to help everyone would be too large, and a manageable list would be too small for the needs of each reader.

Third, I want to avoid bias. Mentioning names could draw you away from other places that might be a great fit.

Finally, searching broadly to develop *your list* and then narrowing it down are important for learning how to make a decision. You can do this. I'll recommend a number of websites with tools to develop a manageable list.

What about alternatives to college?

The steady rise in college costs has led to alternative options. These less-expensive opportunities for job training and education will probably grow, and that already has some people questioning the need for a college degree.

Low-cost options are tempting. There is no harm in exploring them, but most high school graduates with the talent, time, and financial opportunity should still take a traditional college route, unless they find a lower-cost alternative to anchor a foundational life experience, one that comes close to what a college or university with a strong fit would provide.

Viable alternatives to the traditional college path could certainly emerge in the future, but I don't think we're there yet. My primary concern would be missing a broad-based education for life and the range of options for self-discovery.

That said, college is not for everyone. If an alternative proves to be the best route, then do what you need to do. Just think it all the way through before committing to that path.

Habits of Mind for College and Life

SECTION THREE

Section Three Preview

This section covers mental habits and life lessons, all of which fall under the first pillar for a foundational life experience in your college years.

Chapter 15 highlights persistence, commitment to moments that matter, failure, feedback, and the importance of alignment.

Chapter 16 revolves around a long-past wilderness expedition that still provides low-tech lessons for a high-tech world.

Chapter 17 reveals the need for courage in your convictions and healthy competition.

Chapter 18 covers how to defeat anxiety and fear of failure, and applies it to grades and college admissions.

Chapter 19 identifies the universal predictor for success and a key mindset for achieving it.

Chapter 20 offers questions and answers to clarify misunderstandings.

Chapter 15

STELLA!

Commitment, Feedback, Failure, and Alignment

"I've missed more than 9,000 shots in my career.
I've lost almost 300 games. Twenty-six times I've been trusted to
take the game-winning shot and missed. I've failed over and
over and over again in my life. And that is why I succeed."

Michael Jordan, basketball superstar

Habits of mind are fundamental building blocks for your personal and professional achievements. They will drive your college search and decision, the quality of education you receive, and how well you develop transferable skills.

That's why I have to dedicate an entire section to them.

Life Lessons Rhyme

Life lessons can play a key role in shaping mental habits, because they sit at the intersection of knowledge and wisdom, connecting different areas of life with learning and development.

Parts of this book are intentionally random to show how even a comedy like *The Replacements* or the stories and metaphors in this section can still be valuable. The stories to come in the first three chapters of this section are chosen for the lessons they offer, despite happening many years ago.

But that's intentional, too.

Going back in time illustrates that you can learn from reflecting on experiences—good and bad. Wanting to "move on" or minimize something because "it's in the past" can take success for granted or be a weak excuse to avoid the pain associated with past mistakes. Of course, you should avoid obsessing on the past.

It is often said that history doesn't repeat itself, but it rhymes. This line of thought highlights that history has recurring themes. Life lessons rhyme, too. That's why you can use *every experience* to prepare for the future.

Michael Jordan's perspective on how failure leads to success emphasizes the importance of lasting persistence. No doubt, many athletes would agree with Jordan. The same is true for professional actors, so let's see what we can learn from them.

What follows are important mental habits that you will need to excel in college and life.

Post-College Funk

Peter Pan is the boy who refuses to grow up. After graduating and having missed the opportunity for a foundational experience, I was stuck in a post-college funk, clueless about what to do next. The Peter Pan years were on.

It's a long story. The short version is that money saved from high school and college jobs allowed me to buy a small car, drive across the country, and try to flush the funk. In Los Angeles, a friend's roommate was acting in commercials, and suggested I give it a shot. This was one of those random it's-never-too-late-to-learn things. Even better, it delayed driving home without a job or a clue.

How's that for a weak rationalization?

But there were two problems: First, it was hard to find quality acting training. Second, I was the worst table waiter in the galaxy. Seriously, words can't describe how bad. Eventually, I found the

Stella Adler Academy of Acting and Theatre—Los Angeles.[1] It was only established a year earlier in 1985, which was probably the reason I was accepted.

Stella Adler was a legendary teacher whose past students included Marlon Brando and Robert De Niro. Her program was built on fundamentals with a dedicated group of teachers. The program went deeper than others I had seen, which seemed more focused on learning how to smile and otherwise gesticulate in commercials.

Larger Than Life

Although Stella was 85 years old when she founded her L.A. acting school, her mind was still razor sharp. She visited periodically to lead sessions in a small black box theater, during which students performed scenes for her to critique. This was can't-miss stuff. Stella would preside in a large chair next to a side table—lower stage right—and always made a larger-than-life entrance with a raucous ovation from her students.

Stella never held back if she sensed talent in an actor. Nor did she hesitate to stop a scene and jump in. Her critiques, which varied in tone and style, were always professional, never personal. Sometimes she was gentle and other times direct. Or if necessary, she unloaded with high-voltage comments aimed at a breakthrough.

One time, a young woman was struggling on stage. Stella sensed potential and went off. I remember hearing, "You are acting to the words. Just words, words, words . . . the words mean nothing!" Which was followed by something about being false, not believing the actor, and how the actor needed to "lift!" her character to the grand ideas of the play. Stella was right, but we still felt for this young actor facing such an intense critique.

---

1   It was founded originally as the Stella Adler Conservatory of Acting—West.

You may know of two people in the room that day. Benicio del Torro and Mark Ruffalo were classmates with the most raw, unequaled talent in our group. Nobody questioned if they would make it, only when.

Benicio broke through quickly. About three years later, he was on the big screen in *License to Kill* fighting James Bond. His was an early but well-earned breakthrough. Benicio has talent, a work ethic, and the willingness to take risks, which makes him worthy of his long career and Academy Award. You probably know Mark from his Academy Award nominations, such as *Spotlight*, or from playing the Hulk in the Avengers series.

Okay, like my children, you're probably thinking, Where's this going? So what if you took acting classes with future stars who wouldn't remember you? What are the lessons for me?

Fair enough. Here we go.

Feedback and Failure

This story highlights natural learners who try, fail, reflect, and correct. An actor's performance only shows the end product: a Broadway show, television series, or movie. We don't see the hard work, audition rejections, and other emotional struggles that actors must endure. We don't see how successful actors come to understand the paradox that they can't succeed until they fail.

Struggles occur throughout any acting career, and an actors' developmental years can be brutal. They go on stage repeatedly to receive feedback, often negative, from their coaches and peers. There were times when Benicio and Mark faced withering criticism, but they persisted—no matter the emotional challenge—just as you will need to do in college and life.

A huge part of failure and eventual success is getting feedback and correcting yourself. Professional actors and athletes are extreme examples, but everyone has to deal with similar issues. You'll get feedback throughout life, and you won't like all of it.

Truly successful people from all professions welcome feedback, especially when it's something they need to hear. They don't blow off disagreements or—and this is really important—surround themselves only with people who agree with them.

The most common way people reject negative feedback is to ignore it. And those who can't get past unhealthy competitive behaviors often "shoot the messenger" by demeaning the person giving them negative feedback or blowing it off as someone "hating on" them. This is just denial, and it's a big problem. When most people take time to give you feedback—be it good or bad—they're giving it to help *you*.

The expression "feedback is the breakfast of champions" exists for a reason. It's your responsibility to choose how it's received.

- Do you listen, sort through what you need to hear, and try to improve?
- Do you work only on the easy fixes?
- Or, do you reject it?

How you react to feedback is an important mental habit—one that will go a long way to fulfilling your potential in college and life.

Finally, I hope you see why it's pointless to fear failure or obsess over perfection. The only abject failure is the failure to learn from mistakes. That's it. Without failure, we can't succeed.

Deep Commitment

Let's look at what Stella really meant in her critique of the young actor and how it applies to life.

Most people would think Stella was trying to say, "Actions speak louder than words," which is true to an extent. She was always keen on the deliberate choices actors made with their appearance, actions/

reactions, and other movements on stage. But she wanted more from them, much more.

Stella wanted *a deep commitment to the moment*. Deep enough for the actor's real self to be lost in the important ideas of the play, the time and place depicted in the play, and the soul of the character the actor portrays. Without this deep commitment, Stella saw false moments, which she thought would leave an audience in disbelief.

Let's be clear, though: I do *not* mean you should become obsessed with a grand goal or idea. Everyone needs balance.

Deep Commitment in the Real World

Stella encouraged all actors to be "students of life," so it's important to see how her deep commitment to the moment works in the real world. For example, you've seen many teachers in action—good, bad, and average. Take a minute to remember the teachers (or coaches) you think are exceptional. Beyond high skill levels, what makes them special? What separates those who are exceptional from those who are good?

Since I don't know any of the teachers you're thinking about, what follows is an experienced guess.

Your exceptional teachers have the same deep commitment to important moments that Stella wanted from her actors. They don't have false moments. When you interact with them, you sense they care deeply about you, even if they're disciplining you. They focus on learning and make the effort to reach out when you need help. You feel they are tuned into you in ways other teachers are not. Finally, they bring out your best because you want to equal their commitment, energy, and focus.

Every profession has times when a deep commitment is necessary—just as there will be similar moments throughout your personal life.

Alignment

Here's another big lesson from Stella. When she critiqued the young actor, Stella said, "You are acting to the words. Just words, words, words . . . the words mean nothing!"

Stella knew the words meant something—of course she did—but she wanted *alignment* first. She thought an audience only believes what they see if the big ideas of the play line up with the soul of the character and the choices an actor makes on stage.

Alignment was fundamental to Stella's teaching. This is how she thought actors gave meaning to their words. And alignment isn't limited to acting. It's fundamental to making quality decisions—proceeding through the Big Picture to Middle to Final phases. It also matters when following through on a big decision.

Alignment in the Real World

Imagine making an important decision, for example, to become a doctor or an engineer, which will be an ongoing challenge that takes focus and stamina—day after day, month after month, year after year. Stella's belief in alignment can help you achieve a major goal by keeping your thoughts aligned with your actions, just as she demanded of actors.

Think about how many obstacles you'll face when trying to reach a long-term goal. Ups and downs, unexpected challenges, and other distractions can knock you out of alignment. Your commitment will be tested with temptations to rationalization an easier path or bail out on your original decision.

When in doubt, try to remember this cornerstone of Stella's teaching: Alignment is truth. Misalignment is false.

Persistence: A Long Day's Journey to the Hulk

Mark Ruffalo's career exemplifies persistence and alignment. Acting is a high-risk professional decision. For every actor who has a long career, there are thousands who barely get by or have to move on to other pursuits. If you have a deep passion for a risky career and you're certain you need to go for it, then do it, but keep your expectations grounded. Know what you are sacrificing to pursue a risky route, and step back periodically to assess your situation.

Mark must have doubted himself. He needed about six hundred auditions over fourteen years to land his breakthrough movie role in *You Can Count On Me* .[2] Think about being rejected six hundred times over fourteen years! That's a lot of failure. At any point, he could have been knocked off course, but he stuck with alignment for acting and life.

Find a Romulan Commander

Finally, let's return to post-college funk, which is a real thing. It's not quicksand, so there's no need to panic. It's just being stuck. While the years after college tend to be ripe for it, everyone has times when they feel stuck and have no idea of what they should do.

If you're stuck before, during, or after college, try to remember it's just a phase, and what sets you free can be completely unexpected. In my case, the credit goes to Joanne Linville, who in her acting days played a Romulan commander on the original *Star Trek* television series . (For you Trekkies, it's season 3, episode 2.)

Joanne was a cofounder and instructor at the Stella Adler Academy. Through no fault of her own, she taught me more about teaching than acting. Joanne's teaching brought the same deep commitment to the moment—time, energy, and focus—that Stella wanted in actors. While everyone else focused on acting, I was distracted by how well Joanne taught her classes. It didn't take long to realize I was far more interested in teaching and coaching than anything else.

---

2   "Mark Ruffalo on Going for Broke," CBS News, November 16, 2004, *https:// www.cbsnews.com/news/mark-ruffalo-on-going-for-broke/2/.*

Acting was fun, but I wasn't close to being into it at a professional level. I *needed* to be a teacher.

This jolt came from nowhere, but that's the point. Keep your eyes and ears open. You never know when something will flip a switch. Thanks to Joanne, Benicio soon battled Bond, Mark began his long journey to Hulk-dom, and Peter Pan started to grow up. Not to mention Joanne's other students who benefitted in countless ways.

Persistence, commitment, feedback, alignment, and learning from failure are mental habits that you can develop. These are critical to a foundational experience in your college years, making strong decisions, following through on them, and succeeding in life—no matter what you pursue.

Chapter 16

40 DEGREES BELOW ZERO

Experiential Learning and Personal Responsibility

> "In the long run, we shape our lives, and we shape ourselves.
> The process never ends until we die. And the choices
> we make are ultimately our own responsibility."
>
> *Eleanor Roosevelt, former First Lady*

Personal responsibility is a life lesson that goes to the core of our choices and decisions. It plays a huge role in learning, too. I also see personal responsibility as a very important mental habit. While some might disagree with this, nobody should question its importance.

So I'll repeat what I wrote in Chapter 2: The degree to which you learn and develop in college and throughout life—both personally and professionally—is driven by the responsibility you take. *Where you go to college will shape your experience, so that's why it matters, but what you achieve in college and later in life comes down to you—no matter where you go.*

If you duck responsibility, you won't like the results.

An Old Story with Age-Old Lessons

When I left Los Angeles and drove home, it was time to get serious about becoming a teacher and coach. It was November and schools wouldn't start hiring until the following spring. My parents were educators, so I knew about the growing importance of experiential learning, an approach in which the teacher steps back to facilitate and guide, while students learn by doing rather than listening to lectures. This might sound normal to you now, but it was just entering classrooms then, and I was warned the technique is harder than it seems.

With time on my side, I signed up for an Outward Bound course that would allow me to learn firsthand about experiential learning, and to be honest, I hoped the course's length would flush any residual post-college funk out of my system.

This leads to an old story about an intense experience in extreme conditions. Maybe that's when I came to see extremes as a good way to learn. As you read this, think about how you would feel and react in this situation—day after day.

- Where does personal responsibility come in?
- What do you notice about how we were learning?
- Would you have found healthy perspectives while facing hardships?

Although this experience happened a long time ago, it still offers many life lessons that are so low-tech artificial intelligence will never wipe them out. And you don't need to be in extreme situations to learn them.

Don't Forget Your Headlamp

It was mid-January in 1988 when a group of young men and women from across the country gathered on a cold, cloudy day in Duluth, Minnesota. We met in the early afternoon for the first time without realizing how much we would learn about life, ourselves, and each other.

Most were still in college. One or two were about to start, and a few, like me, were recent graduates. We loaded our bags into vans, drove north to Ely, Minnesota, and arrived in the dark at Outward Bound's Voyageur School. It was the start of a ninety-day wilderness course built on literal extremes. The first half was based in Ely, and the second was spent desert hiking and canoeing in Texas, near the Mexican border.

After dinner and orientation, we gathered in a cabin, complete with bunk beds and a woodstove. An instructor had us lay our gear on a bed and cross-check it with the packing list we had received. Long underwear? Check. Inner- and outer-gloves? Check. Headlamp? Check...

Next, we were issued the gear Outward Bound provided, which included a sleeping pad to prevent the snow from draining our body heat. We were also handed two sleeping bags: a down-filled inner bag and a thicker, hooded outer bag.

Nerves kicked in when the instructor gave each of us a thin tarp. Apparently, we were going to sleep under these. Most of us were thinking, *Seriously? No tent!* The tarps were pitched with ski poles and tied down. Picture a one-person pup tent without sides. Someone piped up, "The information said overnight temperatures can drop to 20 degrees below zero. Can these tarps handle that?"

The instructor replied with something along the lines of, "Actually, the record low is about 40 degrees below zero. You'll be fine. The tarp keeps frost from building up on you. The pad and sleeping bags keep you warm. We'll show you. *Then, you can figure out what works best for you.* You need to learn how many layers to wear while you sleep and the best way to tie the bag around your head to breathe freely. You don't want cold air slipping into your bag."

Since we all expected a nice night in the cabin, our faces had to be priceless when the instructor told us to pack up. Turns out, we were going to snowshoe for about forty-five minutes to our campsite. Heading out the door, no doubt holding back laughter, she added, "Don't forget your headlamp."

Twist, Squirm, Shift, and Pull

Walking through the dark pine forest on what we would soon consider a warm, 20-degree night is a great memory. The headlamps nar-
rowed our vision but made the snow sparkle. It was Narnia. When
we came to a frozen lake, the instructors walked onto it and dropped
their packs. That's when we realized we were supposed to sleep *on
the lake*! Someone asked about sleeping in the woods. "Sure. But the
lake's flat, it's safe, and there are no branches to trip over."

We learned how to set up our so-called tents and laid out our
sleeping bags. No problem—until we had to get in them. The inner
bag went inside the hooded outer bag, so getting into both was a
twist-squirm-shift-and-pull thing until they were up to our necks.
Then, we had to tie the outer bag hood around our faces, tie the inner
bag over our shoulders, and find a position to sleep without air slipping in. It was a little claustrophobic, until we got used to it.

Of course, I was one of a few brain surgeons who got extra practice. Apparently, it's a good idea to hit the "restroom" before getting
into the sleeping bags. Later, as I finally dozed off, a loud crack went
off next to me as the ice settled, and the shot of adrenaline ramped
my mental blender to hyperspeed: *Oh #@%*! Why am I in a bag on a
frozen lake in Minnesota?!!*

Terrain Dictates

Over the next forty-four days we explored the Boundary Waters Canoe
Area Wilderness, which stretches from Ely across the Canadian border. We carried personal gear in our backpacks, using cross-country
skis that were wider than normal. There was a big canvas tent after
all, but it was used as a warming hut and kitchen, not for sleeping.
Group gear and food was transported by dogsled.

We got up every morning, cooked breakfast, fed the dogs, packed
a lunch and our gear, loaded the sled, and off we went. We trekked
across lake after lake, dealing with whatever Mother Nature threw

at us. We were told our destinations and had to figure out how to get there as a group. On trails between the lakes, we dealt with the unexpected trees, roots, and rocks. Terrain dictated where the sled went, while the instructors stood back to let us figure it out.

At our destinations, we unpacked, set up camp, gathered and chopped wood, and cooked dinner in the big tent. We discussed how the day went and hung out for a while before starting our sleep prep routines. Cell phones hadn't been invented yet. On and on it went with some time at the Ely base camp to resupply, rest, and thankfully, shower.

Learn by Doing

The instructors never compromised our safety. Beyond that, "You'll figure it out," or "What do you think we should do?" were standard replies. It drove us crazy until we understood why they were doing it.

Experiential learning comes from doing. Try, fail, reflect, correct. We always had to assess our success or failure.

- What did we do well? Why?
- What can we do better? How?

The instructors wanted us to be *active learners* who take personal responsibility for our experiences and the lessons we learned. They were direct about being indirect, because self-reliance—individually or as a group—cannot be built by someone else.

Low-Tech Lessons for a High-Tech World

We experienced a beautiful area of the world in ways few people do, and the lessons learned remain valuable. In no particular order, we learned the fundamental importance of:

- how little we actually need to be happy;

- anticipating problems and preparing for challenges that *might* come;
- learning how to agree *and* disagree;
- understanding what matters the most (fancy brand names and other superficial stuff meant nothing when the wind chill dropped);
- personal responsibility and self-reliance;
- finding a healthy perspective, smiling in the face of adversity, and doing what needs to be done (self-pity and whining were useless);
- dealing with uncertainty and accepting imperfection;
- sharing the hard work of leading upfront to break the trail (This makes it easier for the dogs to pull the sled);
- taking time to step back, make practical decisions, and march on; and
- the satisfaction that comes only from hard work and a hot drink.

Most of these lessons were reinforced in a dramatically different environment over the following forty-five days in Texas.

Every one of these lessons will apply throughout your life.

And if you could ask one of the trip instructors where you should go to college, the response would probably be: "You'll figure it out, and I'm happy to help. But don't forget your headlamp."

Chapter 17

CHICKENS AND EAGLES

Conviction and Healthy Competition

> "'There are all kinds of courage,' said Dumbledore, smiling.
> 'It takes a great deal of bravery to stand up to our enemies,
> but just as much to stand up to our friends.'"[1]
>
> *J. K. Rowling, author of the Harry Potter series*

Let's see what chickens and eagles have to do with the mental habits and healthy competitive traits that everyone needs to combat the cultural avalanche. The following story applies to everything in life. It's been helpful as a parent and for guiding others.

When the Baby Eagle Leaves the Nest

This story comes from Howard Cross, who played tight end for the New York Giants from 1989 to 2001. On the field, Howard could run, hit, and catch with the best in the National Football League (NFL). Off the field, he was one of the nicest guys I've ever met.

In the 1990s, I left teaching to attend graduate school and ended up in what was the newly formed Player Programs department at the NFL's New York office. The department was established to help players finish their college degrees, find internships, and prepare for life after football.

---

1   J. K. Rowling, *Harry Potter and the Sorcerer's Stone* (New York: Scholastic, Inc., 1997), 306.

We also piloted an outreach program called the "NFL Effort Honor Roll." The goal was to help urban middle schools provide students with effort-based grades alongside regular grades. We hoped to instill a sense of achievement by giving meaningful recognition to students' hard work. No matter their academic grade, any student who put in *legitimate* effort could earn a place on the NFL Effort Honor Roll.

Howard was among the players I asked to visit schools and speak at assemblies, and what follows is my distant memory of how he began his talks. Howard explained that he grew up in Alabama, where he learned how chickens were raised, and then asked, "Anyone here know how chickens and eagles grow up?" A few in the audience would raise their hands.

"Really? . . . Good! Then you know a baby chicken struggles to get out of its shell. And when it gets out, it's a cute little bird with soft, fuzzy feathers. Is there anybody who doesn't think a little chick is cute?" A *Noooooooooo!* would ring out from the audience. "Soon this chick runs around with the other cute little chicks in a safe little chicken world. The farmers feed them and keep the foxes away. It's great to be a chicken!"

Then he said, "It's not so great to be a baby eagle. They grow up without any protection. The baby eagle struggles to get out of its shell and has to keep struggling. Because when that little eagle comes out, it's awkward and has splotchy feathers. That poor bird can barely do anything and needs its mother to chew food and drop it into her baby's mouth." The audience would react with a collective *Eeeeewwwwww!*

"The baby eagle always takes longer to grow than the baby chicken. It stays in its nest with only a brother or sister eagle for company. The eagle doesn't run with a flock; it has to be patient. It takes time to develop. But when the baby eagle leaves the nest, it soars. The eagle hunts. The eagle becomes a majestic bird.

"You ever see a chicken do that?" *Nooooooo!* "Do you know what happens to the chickens?"

Howard let them throw out ideas. "No. No. No. . . .

The chickens become McNuggets®!" Everyone would laugh and Howard always had captivated the room.

"So do you want to be a chicken or an eagle?" Shouts of *Eagle!* would fill the room. "Great! Let's talk about the effort it takes to become an eagle...."

Peer Pressure Never Goes Away

Howard's chicken and eagle story is terrific for middle schoolers. It meets them at their level and helps them avoid the negative influences of peer pressure. To give their full effort in school, even if others are doing less. To understand there's nothing to apologize for if they need to be different or do something in a different way.

As you approach the end of high school, you've probably heard these messages many times, but you might not have heard that peer pressure never goes away. Direct verbal pressure might come less frequently, but the cultural avalanche builds, the sense of competition rises, and the pressure to "keep up" can result in status anxiety.

While many lessons can be drawn from Howard's story that go beyond school, I want to focus on healthy versus unhealthy competition and the importance of having the courage of your convictions.

Healthy competition allows you to excel while avoiding the toxicity of unhealthy competition. Howard's story highlights sharp differences between chickens and eagles, and I'll use extremes again to explore competitive traits—a worst-case example followed by an ideal.

Although rare, there are people with strong habits of mind who can live up to the healthy ideal at every moment, and there are people with mental habits that trap them in unhealthy extremes. The rest of us form the vast majority whose healthy or unhealthy competitive traits come out depending on the situations we're in.

As you read, try to think of times when you came close to the ideal and others that pulled you toward negative extremes.

Unhealthy Competition

Do you know people who are overly self-critical or constantly make petty judgments of others? These are the scoreboard watchers, who obsess over how well they're doing in comparison to others. Their lack of perspective means if one person is winning, then others must be losing, and if they fall too far behind, their mental blenders ramp up. They knock themselves down or try to tear down others; sometimes both. They also think in simplistic ways, slapping easy labels on people and situations: yes or no, good or bad, winner or loser.

How often do you see people display insecurity when they want approval from others? Obviously, everyone needs approval to know, for example, if their work is up to an expected standard. But going overboard with a constant need for validation is unhealthy. At the extreme, this quest for approval turns people into Olympic-caliber butt kissers. You know the type. These are the people who always tell others, especially those in authority, what they want to hear.

It's also a two-way street. The recipients who don't shut this down are equally unhealthy. They're so enamored by what they want to hear, they never get what they need to hear.

These insecurities often push people to ignore fundamentals and go with style over substance. Instead of real achievement, they look for a shortcut by running with the cool kids, fooling themselves into thinking that an association with brilliant people or big brand-name organizations will convince others they have the same brilliance and reputational excellence.

Finally, many unhealthy competitors struggle with adversity. If they feel successful in impressing people, they'll continue to pursue a goal. Yet, when a goal takes more time, effort, or adversity than expected, they fear that other people will look more successful. Instead of grinding through obstacles, they convince themselves it's time to quit and pursue something else.

Why?

For unhealthy competitors, *appearing successful* is more important than the work it takes to achieve real success.

Healthy Competition

Healthy competition goes hand in hand with healthy perspectives. Think about runners who measure success by their personal best times, not how they finish in comparison to others. Doing so allows them to compete internally—to run their own race. They run at their pace and avoid burning out from the must-keep-up intensity of the race. They focus on *the process* instead of immediate results and perform to the best of their abilities.

People like this have patience and a strong sense of balance. They know when to push harder and when to back off, no matter what other people think, say, or do. *Since there's always another race to run, they know their performance levels will improve with time and effort, and that will lead to their best results.*

People with the healthiest competitive traits also take joy in others' success. They are immune to relative deprivation, because they see their lives as a personal journey, sticking to a path that fulfills *their* potential. They also understand why Dale Carnegie pointed out that birds and horses are happy because they aren't trying to impress the other birds and horses.

I know chickens are birds, but you get the point.

Healthy competitors have goals and push themselves, but they hold realistic expectations. While they have the same demands from families, careers, and friends as their unhealthy counterparts, they are just as productive, if not more so.

When Dorothy Wakes Up

It's easy to say Howard's eagles all grow up to have healthy perspectives on competition, but the journey is not easy. Personal development is a never ending work in progress, and it's always difficult to defy cultural gravity. For example, simplistic labeling and a desire for approval are drummed into us at an early age. In the *Wizard of Oz*, when Dorothy wakes up after the tornado transports her to Oz, she's asked immediately if she's a "good witch or a bad witch."

This type of labeling and focus on approval starts everyone on a path to unhealthy competition, which, left unchecked, warps our choices and decisions.

- How many students choose a college to impress others?
- How many people let others determine their happiness and sense of self?
- Do you really want to make a life-altering decision because it will sound good at a cocktail party?

And Dorothy's response: "I'm not a witch at all. I'm Dorothy from Kansas." She's an eagle.

The Courage of Your Convictions

We've established that everyone's decisions are tested, and the reasons why you make them need to hold up to challenges. This leads to the courage of your convictions—acting in alignment with your beliefs, especially in the face of unfair or unhealthy criticism from others.

If you make decisions that go against the grain of commonly held beliefs, you should expect some backlash, because other people might see what you do as challenging their beliefs. When Jeff Bezos laid out his ambitious and aggressive plans for Amazon in the 1990s, many of his business peers thought he was nuts. For years, he was hit with gratuitous, and sometimes personal shots from the "cool kids." Still, he had a great idea and the courage of his convictions to see it through.

How did that work out for the cool kids?

Bezos's advice to those who go against the grain is this: "Me-too companies have not done that well over time. So you need to invent and *be willing to be misunderstood.*"[2] A few of you will need to make college decisions that go against the grain. Are you prepared to deal with family, friends, and others who might not take time to understand? How about future life decisions they don't understand?

This chapter begins with a quotation from J. K. Rowling, who believed in herself when others didn't. She was an unemployed single mother on government assistance while writing *Harry Potter and the Sorcerer's Stone.* It took serious conviction on her part to see it through. She battled the cultural stigma attached to single mothers, stuck to her goal, and surely had doubts along the way. Thankfully, she had the courage of her convictions, even after twelve publishers turned down her manuscript.

You might be thinking, "But these are exceptional people." They are. Without question. Except, that's not an excuse to rationalize your way out. With over seven billion people on the planet, it's probably safe to say at least a billion have the courage of their convictions.

Why?

---

2   Rob Verhuel, "How to Innovate Like Amazon: 7 Principles you Can Apply to Shake Up Your Industry," Graphite.com, June 29, 2018, *https://www.graphitedigital. com/blog/how-to-innovate-like-amazon-7-principles-you-can-apply-to-shake-up-your-industry.*

Ordinary people do extraordinary things every day. They just don't get the recognition famous people do.

Groups Still Matter

Finally, Howard's story is not meant to question the value of groups. "Eagles" still need others to succeed. Of course, their groups—friends, coworkers, employers, and the organizations they work with—should be chosen carefully.

When adults choose style over substance, what they really want is the comfort and approval that comes from their groups. Healthy competitors stand apart, if necessary. Even within a group, there are times when you must see, think, and act like an eagle.

Run *your* race.

Chapter 18

THE ELEPHANT DIET

How Effort and Circumstantial Reinforcement Conquer Stress

This chapter brings us back to fear of failure and addresses the biggest lesson from Howard Cross' story about chickens and eagles, which I'll relate to grades and college admissions. Then, we'll see how a concept I call *circumstantial reinforcement* can defeat stress and anxiety.

A Gateway Condition

Perspective determines how well you handle stress, because how you choose to view failure will either wind you up or calm you down. Remember, I'm defining "failure" loosely, as anything between falling short of a goal to utter failure—falling flat on your face.

Although face plants are rare, fear of failure still runs rampant and triggers stress, which means it serves as a gateway condition to other problems. However, a healthy perspective cuts off many issues before they become worse.

Just the hint of failure throws too many people off. They're afraid to commit to anything that *might* be a waste of time and energy—or worse. Learning from failure rarely occurs to them. And even if they do commit fully, fear of failure still chips away at their convictions.

This leads many people to make commitments, but only with minimal effort, which provides a convenient excuse when things don't work out. We've all done this at some point. Be honest. I have and you have, too. But this half-a-loaf approach is just baked-in failure.

The obvious solution is simple, but hard: don't do it.

Take the Leap and Play Hard

To avoid the half-a-loaf trap, let go of anxiety and focus instead on your best effort. Howard always pointed out that eagles fly and chickens don't. That's where the big lesson is found:

When eagles launch, they take a leap of faith every time.

Flying might be routine to an eagle, but there are never guarantees, so it always takes a leap of faith whenever they launch. Notice that eagles don't hope they will fly; they have faith they will fly. Hope is a nice feeling, but it's fleeting, while faith is stronger and lasts longer. When the wind chill drops hard and fast, faith outlasts hope.

In the real world, "eagles" put faith in their best effort. And why not? No one knows if real eagles fear failure, but we do know the cost of failing in flight is far worse than a bad grade, not getting into a dream college, or almost any other setback.

If you have devout religious beliefs, you probably feel strongly that your faith should be placed in God. There's nothing wrong with that. But remember, God still wants your best effort.

Do the best you can in the time you have, because the only failure worthy of fear is the failure to launch.

When Grades Have Little Meaning

Let's apply this concept to school grades through the following perspective: *Stressing over grades is a complete waste of time and energy.*

Since that just lit every box checker's hair on fire, we better see if it holds up. Think about these questions:

- What do grades represent?

- What matters the most about grades?
- When do grades have value?

Grades measure where you are at a single point in time—nothing more and nothing less. Even semester and yearly grades only measure a fixed time period in your life. Not forever. The same is true for SAT/ACT scores and other standardized tests. There's no reason you can't do better in the future, and you might do worse.

The point is that a single test or semester grade will *not* determine your future. None of that means grades are useless. Rather, grades have value when they accumulate to reveal a true measure of strengths and weaknesses. Of course, that only happens with your best effort.

For example, if you want to be a rocket scientist, then your grades will offer important feedback on whether it's the right path. *Over time*, if you give your best effort in math and physics courses, but your grades aren't strong enough, then you should find a different career.

While that reasoning is easy to follow, too many people miss the opposite idea. Grades without genuine effort only give weak information to make life-altering decisions. If you have a passion for rocket science and don't give a good-faith effort, then you'll probably end up with grades that rule out this career.

And that's a serious problem, because *you'll never know if your best effort meant you could have done it.*

Either way, the importance of a good-faith effort should be clear. Any day-to-day focus on grades (immediate results) is misplaced, because your day-to-day effort is what matters the most. Without it, cumulative grades won't measure where you are, what you need to improve, and what you can do in the future.

Here's the same concept applied to college admissions.

College Admissions

As noted in Chapter 2, many students and parents see college admissions as a game. That's a cynical view, but you can still play this game. Go for it. Compete! But always compete in a healthy way: focus on fundamentals and achievement rather than checking boxes.

Play hard. Play the game the right way. Then, whatever happens will happen. And you are highly likely to end up at a college where you belong, at this point in your development. The last thing you should want is to end up where you don't belong.

"But, what about . . ."

I understand. It's hard to stop worrying. So again, it's pointless to stress over your best effort—be it college admissions, grades, or anything else. The result can't be any better. Your best effort will be nothing less than . . . your best effort . Period. So, have faith in it.

Short- and Long-Term Stress

College is a time of great excitement, joy, challenge, and accomplishment. Getting in, moving up to college-level coursework, living away from home, etc., can be stressful. Just going through college admissions is daunting. You have to maintain your normal workload while finding time to prepare for and take the SAT or ACT, search for colleges, and complete applications.

It's normal if this causes a pit in your stomach. But if you don't address the pit or other anxious feelings, these could suck you into quicksand. Always remember that millions of students have managed the move up to college. And you will, too.

There's also no need to fear short-term or *low-level* stress. Without some seventh-level state of Zen, it never goes away—and that's good. Short-term stress gets you going, maintains your focus, and pushes you to a higher performance level.

Long-term stress is the real problem. Most people link low pressure to a lighter workload and high pressure to a heavier one. So work takes the blame for pressure/stress/anxiety. Except, that's not necessarily true.

Here's another counterintuitive thought: *work and effort actually relieve pressure.*

Think about it. If you don't work hard and stay true to fundamentals, then deep down you know there *will* be consequences. You know something is coming, and it's probably going to be difficult. Even worse, you don't know when. So that drip-drip-drip feeling of angst—be it conscious or unconscious—will only ramp up your long-term stress and anxiety.

The best way to defeat the drip is advice that has been around long enough to become a cliché. It seems simple and obvious, but it works.

The Elephant

In most cases, if you're flipping out over a ton of work or stressing over a big goal like college admissions, you're just creating an elephant in your mind. The longer you worry, the bigger the elephant gets.

Everyone knows this feeling. The root cause is usually a poor perspective that distracts you from what matters the most: stepping back to assess what needs to be done, breaking down the workload or goal into doable chunks, and getting started. If you're stuck and the elephant keeps growing, it's important to admit *you* are the reason. Step back, acknowledge the frustration, and then shrink it.

Eat the elephant!

With a clear head, figure out what needs to be done and do it— one bite at a time. The first piece leads to the next one, and the next one. Soon, your mental elephant will begin to shrink.

Circumstantial Reinforcement

This concept of eating the elephant is built around something I've always called *circumstantial reinforcement*—using small actions to improve your immediate circumstances. Instead of fretting about what you have to do or what might go wrong, you can build confidence through action. As small, real accomplishments build, they add up to greater success. And that will be true throughout life—no matter what you do or how successful you become.

Circumstantial reinforcement is far more effective than positive reinforcement, which the self-esteem crowd has pushed for decades. You know this routine. Everyone is told they're special. Everyone gets a trophy. Everyone feels great. And everyone sees through it, except for the adults pushing it.

Self-esteem is important. Of course it is. But it doesn't take long for constant praise to become hollow and distract from what really matters: circumstantial reinforcement. Doing something—no matter how small—that immediately improves your circumstance, followed by the next small action, and the next one.

Make the Bed

One of the best examples of circumstantial reinforcement comes from William McRaven, a former Navy Seal who rose through the ranks to become a four-star admiral and commander of all U.S. Special Forces. When Admiral McRaven gave the 2014 commencement address to the graduating class of the University of Texas at Austin, he had no idea the speech would go viral.

Here's the key part that relates to circumstantial reinforcement:

"If you make your bed every morning, you will have accomplished the first task of the day. It will give you a small sense of pride and it will encourage you to do another task and another and another. By the end of the day, that one task completed will have turned into many tasks completed. Making your bed will reinforce the fact that little things in life matter. . . . And, if by chance you have a miserable day, you will come home to a bed that is made—that you made—and a made bed gives you encouragement that tomorrow will be better."[1]

It's that simple. Make your bed. There's no angst or other needless drama—just a small action that improves your circumstance by taking you from a messy bed to a well-made one. Admiral McRaven's speech and a book he wrote afterwards can be found by searching for "McRaven Make Your Bed."

Have faith in your best effort. Do the best you can in the time you have. Play hard. Play the game the right way. If you can do that as part of a foundational experience in your college years, you'll be well on your way to achievement and a fulfilling life.

---

1   William H. McRaven, *Make Your Bed*, (New York: Grand Central Publishing, 2017), 111.

Chapter 19

YOU CAN'T STEAL FIRST BASE
The Universal Predictor for Success

"One of the things I want people to take away from me, or my personality of ski racing . . . is to stop shying away from their ambition, and to actually face it head on, and work toward it. Because too many people just say, 'No, that sounds crazy. I couldn't even do that.' And then they stop. And what's the point of that?"[1]

Mikaela Shiffrin, American Olympic skier and gold medalist

Stop or persist? It's a universal question for every goal. It's so easy to stop and so hard to persist, which is why people look for a secret to success—anything to make it easier.

Beyond our freedom to define success, the next closest thing to a secret would be the universal *predictor* for success. We've come close to this element several times. Now, we can nail it down by looking at the work of Dr. Angela Duckworth from the University of Pennsylvania and Dr. Carol Dweck of Stanford University. Both reveal important mental habits everyone should pursue.

This chapter starts with Duckworth, whose research found that grit is the most commonly shared element among successful people. Grit has become a go-to word in the past decade. Most people use the term to express what one of my coaches used to call "stick-to-it-ive-ness," but Duckworth's discovery goes beyond that

---

1   2018 Winter Olympics Primetime Broadcast, NBC, Peongchang, South Korea, February 14, 2018.

conventional wisdom. Then, we'll look at a very important mindset Dweck discovered.

Stamina

Duckworth has a popular six-minute TED Talk, which can be found by searching "Angela Duckworth: The Key to Success? Grit." I encourage you to watch it. She's also written a book called *Grit: The Power of Passion and Perseverance.*[2]

Duckworth worked in management consulting before becoming a seventh-grade math teacher in New York City, where she realized some of her smartest students weren't doing as well as others. That led her to ask, "What if doing well in school and in life depends on much more than your ability to learn quickly and easily?"

This simple question pushed her to become a psychologist, examining children and adults across various "super-challenging settings." In each case, she asked who is "successful here and why?" Her research included contestants in the National Spelling Bee, first-year teachers in troubled urban schools, cadets starting at the United States Military Academy, and corporate salespeople.

Duckworth determined that grit is a "significant predictor of success." As she explains in her TED Talk, "Grit is passion and perseverance for very long-term goals. Grit is having stamina. Grit is sticking with your future, day in and day out. Not just for the week. Not just for the month, but for years and working really hard to make that future a reality. Grit is living life like it is a marathon not a sprint. . . . talent doesn't make you gritty."[3]

---

2   Angela Duckworth, *Grit: The Power of Passion and Perseverance* (New York: Scribner, 2016).

3   Angela Duckworth, "Grit: The Power of Passion and Perseverance," TED Talks Education, TED.com, April, 2013, *https://www.ted.com/talks/angela_lee_duckworth_grit_the_power_of_passion_and_perseverance?language=en.*

So there you go. Grit! It's good old-fashioned "stick-to-it-ive-ness" *combined* with passion. Giving your best effort over the long haul, while doing something you enjoy.

I hope you see the irony: Angela Duckworth needed grit to discover grit. It worked for Mark Ruffalo, and I'll bet grit worked for J. K. Rowling and Jeff Bezos, too.

Patience

We can't ignore the role patience plays in sustaining grit. Results—the big ones you really want—do not come quickly. If they do, then it's probably luck or you set the bar too low.

Success has many variables—no one would dispute this—but no matter what you pursue or how you define success, it takes grit to get there. If you want to be an architect, accountant, engineer, nurse, doctor, small business owner, or anything else, you need grit to become one *and* to excel throughout your career.

Finally, there's no need to fear to grit. What you need is the leap of faith that your best effort produces your best results over time. You can do that.

A Growth Mindset Shreds Box Checking

The right mindset is very important to sustaining grit. Carol Dweck's book, *Mindset: The New Psychology of Success*, explores two frames of mind she discovered through research.

Dweck explains, the *"growth mindset* is based on the belief that your basic qualities are things you can cultivate through efforts. Although people may differ in every which way—in their initial talents and aptitudes, interests, or temperaments—everyone can change and grow through application and experience." She adds, "The passion for stretching yourself and sticking to it, even (or especially) when it's not going well, is the hallmark of the growth mindset. This is the mindset that allows people to thrive during some of the most challenging times in their lives."[4] Don't miss "The passion for stretching yourself."

Dweck also explains the opposite: "Believing that your qualities are carved in stone—the *fixed mindset*—creates an urgency to prove yourself over and over. If you have only a certain amount of intelligence, a certain personality, and a certain moral character—well, then you'd better prove that you have a healthy dose of them. It simply wouldn't do to look or feel deficient in these most basic characteristics."[5]

In other words, a fixed mindset can be a root cause of pressure—the feeling that your chance for improvement is so limited you have to get as many results as you can, as soon as you can. It's a feeling that makes it difficult to run your race.

Dweck has a TED Talk you should watch, which can be found by searching for "Carol Dweck: The Power of Believing that You Can Improve." For our purposes, her talk explains how a growth mindset shreds box checking and other unhealthy competitive traits.

She says: "How are we raising our children? . . . Are we raising kids who are obsessed with getting A's? Are we raising kids who don't know how to dream big dreams? Their biggest goal is getting the next A? Or the next test score? . . . And are they carrying this need for constant validation with them into the future, their future lives? Maybe. Because employers are coming to me and saying we have already raised a generation of young workers who can't get through the day without an award."[6]

As Dweck discovered, when people with growth mindsets have difficulties or get a lower than hoped for grade, they don't quit on

---

4   Carol Dweck, *Mindset: The New Psychology of Success* (New York: Random House, 2006).

5   Ibid.

6   Carol Dweck, "The Power of Believing That You Can Improve," TEDxNorrköping, TED.com, November 2014, *https://www.ted.com/talks/carol_dweck_the_power_of_believing_that_you_can_improve?language=en.*

their goals. Instead they think, *not yet*. They understand development takes time.

This perspective is simple and powerful. Instead of allowing immediate results to cause stress or anxiety, people with growth mindsets focus on future achievement. They understand how learning works and have faith that better results will come. They tap into what Dweck calls the "power of yet" and combine it with grit and circumstantial reinforcement.

At all times, they understand the value of try, fail, reflect, correct.

The Truth About Passion

Finally, we should never overlook the role passion plays in Duckworth's definition of grit. No one should expect long-term success if they don't enjoy what they do, but let's not be naïve. Passion, like everything else in life, takes work *and* a healthy perspective. Passion doesn't lead to eternal bliss. Nor is it possible for everyone to build a career around something they love or will stay passionate about for decades.

But passion can be developed.

Dweck's latest work expands her concept of a growth mindset to interests. Working with Paul O'Keefe from Yale University and Greg Walton, also from Stanford, they found a person's interests (or passions) are not fixed. Rather, they can be developed. You can find a good overview of their work in Olga Khazan's article in *The Atlantic* called "'Find Your Passion' Is Awful Advice."[7]

Similar to her work on learning mindsets, Dweck's later research finds that people with a "fixed theory" operate as if they already have a set of interests, and that means their interests just have to be discovered. They need to *find* their passion. This idea is fueled by the

7   Olga Khazan, "'Find Your Passion' Is Awful Advice," *The Atlantic*, July 12, 2018, *https://www.theatlantic.com/science/archive/2018/07/find-your-passion-is-terrible-advice/564932/*.

belief that everyone has a true calling in life—a genuine passion that, once discovered, means you will love your work so much, it will never feel like work. As if, magically, ditch digging will go away.

But "find your passion!" is just more dangerous, feel-good advice—another false narrative in the cultural avalanche. Why? The passion crowd is falling for what they want to hear. They want a warm and fuzzy feeling as they hug the soothsayers and go forth joyfully in search of their life's passion.

Until reality sets in—when they realize they've been job hopping for the last five years along with a six-month stretch on a beach in Bali. Somehow, this was the way they were supposed to find their true selves.

Developed Versus Found

Instead, Dweck and her colleagues' research suggests that *interests can be developed*. There's a big difference between developed and found. Their research discovered that people trying to "find their passion" are too willing to eliminate possible new interests. In the quest for passion, their fixed-theory makes them less likely to fight through obstacles.

That can be a huge problem.

When passion seekers hit tough times, they tend to think what they're doing must not be their passion, which cuts off their desire to persist. However, people who operate with a "growth theory" understand passion can be developed. They don't try to find themselves, they try to develop themselves. They experiment, explore, and dive deeply into *possible* interests. And since learning the fundamentals of anything new never comes easily, they know this takes time.

Why do they persist?

They understand what we covered about happiness and fulfillment in Chapter 3. I'll repeat what's written there: ". . . you strive to reach personal and professional goals by excelling at what you do, because excelling makes you feel good. Deep down, you get the inner satisfaction from overcoming obstacles and pushing past what you had thought were limitations."

Don't try to find your passion; develop it. Of course, everyone should avoid banging their head against a wall, so there is a time to move on. The point is not to bail too quickly when you hit turbulence.

Grow and Evolve

If you have a growth mindset, that's great. But most of us, myself included, are a mixed bag. There are times when we use a growth mindset and other times when we regress to a fixed one. The good news is we can change; we don't have to see all situations in school, work, relationships, activities, etc. as fixed. We can grow and evolve.

In fact, you already used a growth mindset when you learned to walk, run, read, and speak. You weren't born knowing how to do any of these. You had to learn and persist.

You Can't Steal First Base

Life always offers choices and decisions, and it's best to think about the long term. Will it be better to develop grit and learn how to do something really well, or cut corners to get what you want? Should you take the growth mindset and achievement approach or settle for box checking?

Softball and baseball each have shortstops, but shortcuts are not allowed. You always need to get a hit or earn a walk, because you can't steal first base. Yet in college, the number of box-checking students who cut corners to get a degree and land their first job might amaze you. You'll be swamped by passion seekers, too.

Success is slippery—even with your own definition. I hope this chapter helps develop the traction you need.

Chapter 20

SOMETIMES THE DOG ACTUALLY EATS YOUR HOMEWORK

Section Three Questions & Answers

What's the best way to keep my thoughts and actions in alignment when I make a decision?

Trust the process and remember a decision doesn't end after it's made. You still have to follow through. The process will help control your emotions and align your thoughts with actions. When tests come, make sure your actions trace back logically to your big-picture reasons—what matters the most.

It takes practice to recognize when you're drifting out of alignment. For now, trust your instincts. The hair on the back of your neck will signal when you drift. You should also take time to reflect on where you are and what you need to do.

But what happens if something unexpected comes up?

Life happens. Sometimes the dog actually eats your homework, your car breaks down, or you get stuck with demands from other activities. On the Minnesota journey, our sled carried critical supplies. When the sled got stuck, we were stuck. While the hills, lakes, and streams were known obstacles, they still brought surprises. Terrain dictates in life, too.

Something unexpected almost always eats into your time and forces adjustments. It just happens. If something unexpected derails your preparation, then a lower than expected grade on a test is okay. It's only one test, and it's over. If you need to be angry or cry, then do it, briefly. Flush the angst out of your system. Then, step back from your emotions and focus on what matters the most.

Did you do the best you could in the time you had? If the answer is yes, move on. If not, figure out what you could have done differently to give your best effort.

Positive results will come as you improve on balancing demands.

How do you define a good-faith effort?

It begins and ends with personal responsibility; you only answer to yourself. When you can look in the mirror and honestly know you did the very best you could in a reasonable amount of time, you've done it. There's no need for regret. Of course, I'm not referring to a half-hearted attempt rationalized as real work. That's just cheating yourself.

Please don't overlook *a reasonable amount of time.*

Playing the game the right way is about fundamentals, ethics, *and* a reasonable amount of time. Extending a grind only works in the short term. Beyond that, you're developing unhealthy expectations, unrealistic work patterns, and poor habits. An occasional night with limited sleep is one thing, but a pattern of sleepless nights isn't good. It's critical to make a good-faith effort within the boundaries of your *current* ability.

What if I can't avoid sleepless nights?

You should avoid them. Your performance level is not permanent. You will run more than one race, which means you will get better over time. But if you burn out, you'll have to slow way down or even stop.

Back to the frozen lakes. Our group's performance level became more efficient each day and so did every individual. By the end, we were crushing it. If you bring your best effort, you will improve, too—in whatever you do.

But what if . . .

There will always be one "what if" after another: What if it rains? What if the coach benches me? What if I don't get the internship? The only "what if" that matters is, "What if you don't fulfill your potential?"

Of course, "what if" plays a key role in planning, so if Plan A doesn't work, you always need to have a Plan B and Plan C as backups.

If this leap of faith is so logical, why don't more people do it?

Fear of failure.

What about success? Grades are really important to success, why should I not care about them?

You should care about grades! Absolutely. *And* you should keep them in perspective. Giving your best effort doesn't always translate to immediate success. True achievement is about succeeding the right way, eventually. Your best effort over time should produce your best results over time. Grades are a by-product of effort that accumulate to provide information for life altering decisions.

But as we've covered, there's a lot more to long-term success than good grades.

What if I keep failing?

You might be setting yourself up for failure. There's no need to fear failure as long as you learn from the experience. However, if there's no progress, then you might have misplaced expectations, and that can be brutal.

Expectations determine where you set the bar for success. Setting a high bar allows you to push yourself, but setting the bar too high sets you up for failure. So we're back to balance. You need to find an expectation level that is both challenging and realistic.

David and Tom Gardner founded The Motley Fool, a multimedia financial services company. Their investment guide for teens makes an important point about expectations: "Happiness equals reality divided by expectations. Think about that for a second. . .It means that the lower your expectations, the greater your chance of happiness. And it means that the higher your expectations and the worse the reality, the less happiness you'll find. . . Paupers truly can be happier than princes."[1]

This concept applies to a lot more than happiness. And no part of it means you should set low goals. It's okay to shoot for a really big goal in the distance, but use a series of realistic, short-term goals to get there. Raise the bar slowly with circumstantial reinforcement.

---

1   David Gardner and Tom Gardner, *The Motley Fool Investment Guide for Teens: 8 Steps to Having More Money* (New York: Simon & Schuster, 2002), 99.

A Foundational Experience and Perspectives for College

SECTION FOUR

Section Four Preview

This section explains how to build a foundational life experience in your college years, followed by college-related issues and perspectives for your search.

Chapter 21 covers the components of a foundational life experience.

Chapter 22 details the three pillars for building a foundational experience.

Chapter 23 offers thoughts on how college majors impact employment and career earnings.

Chapter 24 explores issues around college size and social life.

Chapter 25 deals with applications, a key step to eliminating high stakes, and the Early Decision option.

Chapter 26 profiles the range of colleges and universities.

Chapter 27 addresses important considerations for the cost of college, including future earnings, sources to help with financial aid, and more.

Chapter 28 provides questions and answers.

Chapter 21

GET YOUR HANDS DIRTY

Components of a Foundational Life Experience

Planning for an uncertain future can lead to feeling stuck. What's right today could be different tomorrow. Or, too many options can be overwhelming. Either case should highlight the need to avoid post-college funk by maximizing your college years through a foundational life experience that will *position and prepare* you for opportunities.

The three pillars for a foundational life experience were introduced in Section One:

Pillar I: Habits of Mind

Pillar II: Education for a Profession and Life

Pillar III: Transferable Skills

The next chapter will cover how to apply habits of mind and develop transferable skills, along with what you'll need for a quality education. This chapter looks at the options available during your college years, building a network, and the need to be intentional in what you do.

Components of a Foundational Life Experience

You do not have to do everything on the list below to have a foundational life experience during your college years. Less can be more. Doing less might produce fewer results, but focusing more intensely on what you do can lead to better, more lasting results.

Here is a general list of components:

- courses (core curriculum for graduation, requirements for a major, and electives);
- service learning/community service;
- student activities;
- study abroad/school-sponsored trips;
- research with a professor;
- a capstone experience (a culminating project that integrates classroom learning with outside experiences);
- a gap year;
- athletics (varsity, club, or recreational);
- independent living (away from home);
- off-campus jobs while enrolled in classes;
- summer jobs/professional internships; and
- work/study on-campus jobs.

It's best to think of this list as a menu to choose how you will accelerate your personal and professional growth.

A balanced plan will combine the elements you need to build on strengths and improve weaknesses. There is no formula beyond balance—developing yourself equally across the three pillars.

It's easy to get wrapped up in campus life and lose sight of the opportunity summers provide. Yet, summer jobs or more formal professional internships should be part of any multi-year plan. These offer the opportunity to:

- gain work experience and develop technical job skills;
- develop your mental habits and transferable skills in professional situations; and
- explore professional interests.

Similar benefits are found through on-campus employment, or student activities that help explore personal interests.

Many colleges and universities have improved their career preparation by integrating internships and other career services with academic programs. This is likely to continue, which means it has never been easier to build a foundational experience across your college years.

A Framework

Self-discovery is key to personal development, and changing your mind is a natural part of that process. There's nothing wrong with a plan that uses the early years of college to figure out what you want to do. That still takes planning along with an understanding of your peaks and valleys—academic, personal, and professional.

A strong plan will be realistic and firm, but still flexible. Your goals can solidify over time. It's best to think of initial plans as *a framework* for what you want to do over the four- to six-year period: potential majors, elective courses, internships, jobs, extracurricular activities, etc.

Your framework should be structured in two stages:

→ **Stage One** focuses on exploring personal and professional interests to determine what you need/want to do professionally.

→ **Stage Two** is a deep dive—when you begin to master the fundamentals for a profession, while still advancing your personal development.

Even if you're certain about a profession or major, Stage One will test your thinking, confirm what you want to do, or help to find something better. Trust the process. There's no need to rush such an important decision.

Paralysis of Choice

Feeling frozen by choices can become the biggest roadblock to deciding on a profession for Stage Two. Although your first career path is a big decision, whatever you decide is still your *first* career path. It's okay to have a few false starts or make a career switch later in life.

Your first career will teach you how to excel at something. There's no need to hold back or hedge your efforts, even if there's a good chance of changing your mind later. Just go for it. *Learn what it takes to perform to a professional standard.* If you switch careers, then what you learn about pursuing excellence in your first career will transfer to the next.

Gap Year Considerations

A gap year is when students take time off from formal education to pursue other activities. This is common in Europe, but largely underutilized in the United States. Traditionally, most gap years happen between high school and college, except there's no rule. Nor is there something wrong with taking time to figure out what you want to do, either before or during college.

Done well, a gap year provides invaluable time for different experiences, reflection, maturity, and self-discovery.

Some students use gap years to bolster their college applications, which might include a few local courses to improve weaknesses or explore new areas of study. Some students use a gap year to gain work experience. Others build in travel or service programs to experience different places, cultures, and activities, while some mix all of these together.

Only take a gap year with clear goals, a strong plan for the full year, and the self-discipline to see it through. This should also fit within your broader plan for a foundational life experience. If you're interested in learning more, Jeffrey Selingo's book *There Is Life After College*[1] has a strong chapter on gap years.

---

1   Jeffrey Selingo, *There Is Life After College* (New York: HarperCollins, 2016).

A few readers might think it would be cool to chill for a year. Yes, it's fun to think about, but don't do it. A little clueless flotation can help with self-discovery, but too much ends in regret.

The University of Manual Labor

The following is only my opinion, but please hear it out. Spending *at least* a summer or half of a gap year at "the University of Manual Labor" is a good option. Manual labor is defined broadly here to encompass any job that keeps you on your feet most of the time.

This is old-school advice because fancy internships and special programs are seen as today's gold standard. Yet, tremendous value remains in any experience where you:

- learn to put in a shift;
- get your hands dirty;
- work forty hours per week; and
- push through sore muscles with a smile.

There is dignity in this work. It should *never* be looked down upon.

Everything in life is a learning experience, and you can develop a number of skills in any job, even those with so-called menial tasks. Furthermore, *if any college admissions committee or future employer holds old-fashioned labor against you, then it's not worth going to that school or joining that workplace.*

Build a Diverse Network

Chapter 11 covered the importance of everyone's information, beliefs, and interests (IBI) and noted that college offers a tremendous opportunity to build your IBI. While everyone's IBI is unique, it still requires other people to develop. And that dovetails with building your personal and professional network—another key goal for any foundational experience.

I'm not talking about racking up contacts on LinkedIn. Instead, college offers the chance to develop relationships with students, professors, administrators, coaches, etc., and to forge professional relationships through internships and other employment. *Extroverts*, channel your nature in productive ways. *Introverts*, avoid comfortable bubbles that keep you from developing important relationships.

Networks are important as you start and then manage a career. Within your network, there should be friends and professional mentors to help you learn and provide sound advice. Diversity matters, too. Try to think in terms of cultural/ethnic, socioeconomic, intellectual, generational, religious, *and* political diversity.

Yes, this means there will be times when you have to agree to disagree with others, which is a very important skill that has been grossly neglected in the age of social media. You don't have to be best friends with everyone, but it's possible to establish effective, mutually beneficial relationships with a diverse set of people, across all age ranges, and from all walks of life.

Intentional About Learning

For decades, millions of students have had internships, worked off-campus jobs, taken gap years, and completed other elements for a foundational life experience. However, few people have done these while learning intentionally.

Unintentional is a different story. Most students—even those who floated through like me—can look back on their college years and realize how much they learned in and out of the classroom. But too few can say honestly they were *intentional about learning across all activities.*

Most of what happens in life can prepare you for the future. Planning your college years well and committing to being be an intentional learner will lead to a strong platform that launches you into adulthood.

Chapter 22

PRACTICE TAKES PRACTICE

Three Pillars for a Foundational Experience

"In theory there is no difference between theory
and practice. In practice there is."

Yogi Berra, professional baseball player

Theory and practice have a thorny relationship. Theory is the reason behind why or how we do something. Theory usually sounds great and fits into those comfortable boxes we like to use.

Practice is doing it—putting a theory to work. Since practice is reality, it's always messy. Almost anything that matters in life takes practice—day after day, month after month, year after year. In short, practice takes practice.

Pillar I: Applying Habits of Mind

Life's daily demands and distractions make it difficult to apply strong mental habits constantly. That's why the first pillar of a foundational life experience aims to practice your mental habits in daily life.

Just the nature of some mental habits pose challenges, too. Some, like finding healthy perspectives, are accomplished by stepping back to think things through, while others need to happen in the moment, such as the way you react to situations, people, good/bad news, or anything unexpected. With an understanding of your strengths and weaknesses, improving your mental habits will depend on your willingness to try, fail, reflect, and correct.

Be deliberate in reflecting on what you've done—big and small. Ask yourself:

- What did I do well?
- Why did it go well?
- What can I improve?
- How can I improve it?

These are simple questions that need *honest* and *specific* answers. And the next time a similar situation comes up, the answers should help you think/react in better ways.

Imagine the advantage gained from your college years if you can learn to:

- develop healthy perspectives, especially during setbacks;
- maintain grit and a growth mindset when you struggle in a course, a semester, or job/internship;
- manage the emotional ups, downs, and in-betweens everyone has in college;
- assess yourself honestly and accurately;
- have faith in your best effort to avoid anxiety over grades or results at work;
- bring deep commitment to moments that matter;
- control emotions when you make decisions or come across information that challenges your beliefs/interests;
- prioritize what you need over what you want;
- engage in healthy competition;
- push hard, but relax and recharge when necessary; and
- stick with achievement over box checking.

Keys for Developing Mental Habits

While your habits of mind will be the driving force behind your education and development of transferable skills, nobody thinks perfectly, so there's always room for improvement.

Peaks and valleys are a given, but you're not starting at zero across the board. That means you should draw confidence from the strong mental habits you already have.

It also takes a few good mental habits to develop others. For example, a growth mindset helps to understand that your mental habits aren't fixed, and circumstantial reinforcement helps to appreciate slow, steady progress.

Challenges will come daily and that's okay. When in doubt, use alignment as you look to the big-picture reasons for why your mental habits are so important. Over time, you will handle challenges more effectively, and the confidence you gain from doing that will become clear to you and others.

Pillar II: Education for a Profession and Life

A strong education can be a fundamental pathway to a fulfilling life. Try to get more from your education than just preparing for a job, especially since you might need to switch careers in the future. This is why a college education should focus on professional *and* personal development, through a college's general education (or core) requirements along with electives (courses students choose outside of any requirements).

Every college course has value, even the so-called "fourth course" students take for personal interest. You'll need to prioritize time and energy every semester. It's nearly impossible to give an equal amount to each course, but rather than blowing off your fourth/fifth course as an easy credit, you can still give a best effort in the time you have.

I met a woman who had attended an Ivy League university, played a varsity sport, and aimed to be a lawyer from the first day of college through her law school graduation. In discussing her experience, she freely admitted that her path was driven by a combination of family pressure and the cultural avalanche. But since these pressures combined with playing a varsity sport, she never looked deeply into her career decision. Yet, the art classes she took for fun—those "fourth courses"—turned out to be her most valuable.

Why?

She's now a very happy graphic designer. By the end of law school, the misery finally led her to stand up for what she wanted to do in life.

Take advantage of academic advising to help think carefully about your interests and what courses to take. Ask questions. Research the fundamentals—what you need to know and master to compete for the jobs/career you want. That information can come from your academic advisor, the career services office, and current professionals in the field.

Liberal Arts Versus Career Majors

Try to be strategic in course selections so they fit within your overall plan for personal and professional development. College majors and minors only provide part of the fundamental base for a profession. And if you decide to pursue a professionally oriented major do *not* discount the importance of liberal arts courses (English, history, economics, psychology, social sciences, math, etc.).

While many of the liberal arts don't have direct career connections, they are fundamental to a quality education, through parts of your core graduation requirements and electives. They help develop important skills, including some of the transferable skills we're about to cover. You could also choose a liberal arts subject as a second major or a minor.

Technically skilled professionals still need transferable skills and an education for life. During a visit to a top engineering college, I met faculty who were equally proud of the liberal arts aspects of their work, because of the balance it brought to their students. Later, the president added, "If we want to produce leaders, then they must have communication skills." That's why a primary goal during her presidency was a renewed emphasis on writing.

The cliché that liberal arts courses teach you how to think is true—if you let them. *Learning to think at a high level and make connections across subject areas is valuable for any career.* As someone moves up the career ladder, these skills can help manage complex situations and solve increasingly difficult problems. How? Proper liberal arts courses will develop your transferable abilities to communicate, think critically, and solve problems from different angles.

All of that will translate to your personal and professional life.

If you pursue a liberal arts major, assess how it will apply across several professions. Then, you can acquire professional knowledge and skills through internships, other experiences, and a professionally focused graduate degree. You won't be fed a lot of professional content in the classroom, but knowing that can make you more deliberate in gaining professional development outside of classes.

Pillar III: Developing Transferable Skills

Transferable skills should be central to any foundational experience in your college years. If the goal is to fulfill your potential, these skills are unavoidable. For simplicity, I'll stick mostly to a professional focus.

The same approach for mental habits applies to transferable skills. Be deliberate as you try, fail, *reflect*, and correct.

Skills are generally described as hard or soft. *Hard skills* are technical or physical and relate to specific activities or professions, while *soft skills* relate to how well you think, interact with others, and meet professional standards. Since these apply across professions (and your personal life), I prefer to call them transferable.

In the second chapter of *There Is Life After College*, Jeffrey Selingo explores the evolving economy and what employers want. Among his findings: "Employers are increasingly looking past the degree and the transcript for a set of skills they believe are better markers of success for their new hires." He also notes employers are increasingly searching for recruits outside of elite colleges. Selingo recommends developing a "set of often overlapping skills: *curiosity, creativity, grit, digital awareness, contextual thinking, and humility.*"[1]

You'll find some transferable skills overlap with mental habits.

Engage, Learn, and Prepare

Think about the skills Selingo identifies: you don't need college to develop them. College certainly helps, but employers wouldn't be looking past academic transcripts if they could find enough people with strong transferable skills.

This reveals a two-part problem:

1. Colleges aren't designed to develop a full professional skill set; and

2. Many students overlook the importance of developing transferable skills during their college years.

Colleges and universities provide an education, credentials, and some professional development. *They do not and should not require full job preparation for students to graduate.* Again, professional development is your responsibility.

Fortunately, most colleges offer many opportunities to develop transferable skills.

---

1   Jeffrey Selingo, *There Is Life After College* (New York: HarperCollins, 2016), 37.

College Life

You can develop many skills just by starting college and managing day-to-day situations. The amount of unstructured time is a huge difference between high school and college. You've generally been told what to do and when to do it throughout your K-12 education, especially if you're involved in after-school activities.

In college, though, you'll be responsible for structuring how to spend much more of your time. Some of you might need to work to pay for college, which provides another opportunity to develop skills. In this case, the job is an important part of your foundational experience. And no matter the situation, finding time to reflect and learn will be critical throughout your college years.

The following list of skills might be intimidating to a high school student. (Actually, the list can intimidate accomplished professionals, too.) But there's no need for fear. Like mental habits, *you're already on a path to developing many of these skills*. The real fear should come from missing opportunities to develop these skills in different situations.

Here are transferable skills you can develop in college and throughout life:

<u>Personal/Interpersonal</u>

- Ability to work in a team
- Adaptability to change and uncertainty
- Listening
- Knowing when to compromise
- Emotional control/attitude/demeanor (can you smile in the face of adversity or stay calm when others lose their cool?)
- Conflict resolution (e.g., dealing with difficult customers, clients, or co-workers)

- Empathy/emotional awareness of others and situations
- Commitment to learning/curiosity
- Ability for professional relationships across age ranges
- Humility
- Patience
- Personal responsibility/taking initiative
- Receiving feedback (positive and negative)

Dynamic Thinking

- Developing healthy perspectives
- Creativity
- Critical thinking (challenge assumptions, understand multiple sides of an issue, assess information and make reasoned judgments)
- Flexibility
- Independent (not susceptible to groupthink)
- Proactive
- Problem-solving
- Strategic

Professional

- Verbal communication (Start by dropping "like" and "you know" —because, like, you know, it drives professionals crazy)
- Written communication
- Ethics
- Organization/planning/time management
- Completing multiple assignments
- Public speaking/presentations

- Technology (ability and understanding)
- Etiquette (behavioral and dress standards)

You don't have to be exceptional at every skill, but you can be good at most. If a definition is unclear, look it up or ask someone.

Finding answers is the first step toward learning.

You can also be creative in learning skills. For example, even an introductory acting class can help. Let's say you're shy and public speaking freaks you out. The right acting class can advance your ability to:

- speak in public without fear;
- adapt to uncertainty;
- control emotions;
- think creatively; and
- work within a team (if there's a performance at the end of the class).

Each skill can then be developed further in other activities or jobs.

Beyond the chance for a great education, your college years offer a terrific time to develop mental habits and transferable skills. A time when you try, fail, reflect, and correct.

Chapter 23

THE REAL JACKPOT

College Majors, Employment, and Career Earnings

> "But there are also unknown unknowns—the ones
> we don't know we don't know."
>
> *Donald Rumsfeld, former U.S. congressman and Secretary of Defense*

When discussing higher education, it's not long before majors, jobs, and salaries come up, and these discussions can lead easily to viewing college as a financial transaction—money spent in return for higher career earnings. Unfortunately, money can cloud the judgment of even the most rational thinkers.

This chapter looks at the following: college majors in relation to careers and predicted salaries; the single greatest difference for career earnings; big-name schools and elite-level earnings; and valuing your college experience.

Majors and Employment

No prior generation has had access to so much information about colleges, majors, and projected salaries. Yet, some of the most irresponsible advice anyone can give a high school senior is to say, "You will earn X amount of dollars, if you choose Y major, and land a job in Z career field."

X to Y to Z sounds simple and logical, but it's a dangerous assumption.

Average or median earnings provide realistic *possibilities*. They are helpful when viewed broadly, except individual results always vary. There's no guarantee you will hit or exceed any average. Most workers entering a field receive salaries that are just above or below the industry's average; however, some salaries fall well below average, while others are well above.

There is also no certainty that a student's career will match their undergraduate college major. The Pew Research Center surveyed workers to learn if their current job relates to their college major or graduate school degree.

Percentage of Graduates Who Say Their Current Job Relates to Their Major in College or Graduate School[1]

Very Closely 49%

Somewhat Closely 20%

Not Very Closely 11%

Not at All 20%

While 69 percent of respondents say their major is "very" or "somewhat closely" related to their current job, 31 percent still end up outside their field of study.

That's a lot of people, and you can't discount the impact of including graduate degrees, because these are usually determined after students have a better idea of what they want to do professionally. That means if only undergraduate majors were used, the unrelated percentages would likely be higher.

Pew points to differences in the way majors and careers align (or not): "Science and engineering majors and, to a lesser extent, those who majored in business are more likely than those who majored in

---

1   "The Rising cost of Not Going to College: Chapter 2: Public Views on the Value of Education," Pew Research Center, February 11, 2014, *http://www. pewsocialtrends.org/2014/02/11/chapter-2-public-views-on-the-value-of-education/*.

the liberal arts, social science or education to say their current job is closely related to their college majors."[2]

But that can be misleading.

It's not uncommon for liberal arts majors to minor in a professional discipline. Or, they major in a liberal arts subject and follow that with a career-focused graduate degree through law, business, or medical school.

As always, what the data doesn't show is important:

- How many of these graduates entered college thinking they would major in one field but switched?
- How many times did they switch?

Clearly, X to Y to Z can be irresponsible advice for high school seniors, and it shows why you should never focus on a single major when searching for a college. Even if you're certain about a great engineering, physical therapy, or interior design program, you still need alternatives in case you change your mind.

Information showing average earnings for graduates from specific colleges, projected earnings for specific majors, and other related click bait floats around cyberspace. But none of that is helpful either.

Here's why.

The Greatest Difference

Your career decision will make the single greatest difference in earnings, by far. Enter a high-paying career—regardless of undergraduate major—and the rest takes care of itself. Thank you, Captain Obvious. Except, it isn't so obvious if you expect high earnings to cover high college loans.

Too many people who anticipate high earnings after college fail to understand a very important point: *high school students still don't know enough about themselves to decide on a future career and count on the*

---

earnings it should provide. It's simply too hard to predict future needs, likes, and dislikes.

Is it realistic to ask teenagers to project what they want to do for work in four to six years? How's that for jumping the process? You might think you want to be a lawyer, doctor, or consultant...*until you don't*. So paying too much for college on the assumption that you'll end up in a high-paying field can lead to a massive problem.

During high school and your early college years, you should never rule out the possibility of a career that pays less, but is much more fulfilling, especially if you're taking out loans.

Ivy League Versus State Schools

Let's challenge the assumption that highly selective institutions lead to elite earnings. Starting in 2011, economists Stacy Dale of Mathematica Policy Research and Alan Krueger of Princeton University did just that with two studies to determine if going to an Ivy League school made a difference in career earnings.

The first study looked at two groups. One group consisted of students who went to an Ivy League school and the other was formed by students who were accepted to an Ivy, but decided to go elsewhere (e.g., Penn State instead of the University of Pennsylvania). The researchers found *no difference* in the average salaries earned over the careers of either group.

That's correct—no difference in money earned. But since all of these students had been accepted to an Ivy, there was little difference in their academic abilities. That prompted the second study, which compared accepted students to those who *applied, but were declined*. Surely, there would be a difference now.

Yet again, there was *no difference* in average annual earnings. It's important to note these studies focused on average salaries, so some students in one group earned higher salaries than those in the other group, and the reverse was also true.

Dale and Krueger's results challenge the idea that the so-called elite schools lead to higher earnings. They conclude: "Our results would suggest that students need to think carefully about the fit between their abilities and interests, the attributes of the school they attend, and their career aspirations."[3] Sounds familiar.

Dale and Krueger did find that African-American, Latina/o, low-income, and students with parents who did not attend college (first-generation attendees) earned more after attending an Ivy compared to those who were rejected. They attribute the differences in career earnings to networking opportunities made possible by these schools—connections their parents and parents' friends could not provide.

Therefore, we can surmise networking (and awareness of possibilities) is important, but doesn't need to happen through a college, unless you come from a traditionally disadvantaged group.

Results of any single research project should be viewed cautiously. Dale and Krueger's work spanned many years. The world has changed since their studies began, and a similar study begun today might show different results in twenty years. But that's not likely to happen.

Why?

The career you choose will make the single greatest difference in your earnings. Where you go to college isn't necessarily going to change your career choice or result automatically in higher pay. K–12 teachers from an Ivy League school still earn the same amount from their school districts as the teachers who go to state colleges and universities, and both earn less than the average doctor or lawyer.

If you're still conflicted about earnings or the ideas presented in Chapter 3 on success in school versus success in life, then check out

3   Stacy Dale and Alan Krueger, "Estimating the Effects of College Characteristics over the Career Using Administrative Earnings Data," *The Journal of Human Resources*, October 19, 2012, *https://www.aeaweb.org/conference/2013/retrieve. php?pdfid=220.*

Frank Bruni's book *Where You Go Is Not Who You Will Be: An Antidote to the College Admissions Mania*.[4]

Balancing Tangible and Intangible Value

The great challenge in valuing a college experience comes down to balancing the tangible and intangible value college provides. Too much emphasis on the financial side (cost vs. projected career earnings) might ignore important intangibles for personal development, but intangibles cannot be ignored.

Your entire college experience will impact how well you launch into adulthood—professionally and personally. The opportunity for self-discovery, personal growth, and maturity should never be taken lightly. The right college will allow you to try new things, think new thoughts, and define yourself as an independent young adult. How do you put a dollar value on that?

There's more to come on college finances, and *nobody should overpay for college*. For now, understand that you can find a place that works financially and still offers these intangibles. It might take extra effort and proper perspective, but it's worth it.

A foundational life experience in your college years is the best way to capture lasting value. Find this at a reasonable cost, and you'll hit the real jackpot.

---

4   Frank Bruni, *Where You Go Is Not Who You'll Be: An Antidote to the College Admissions Mania* (New York: Grand Central Publishing, 2016).

Chapter 24

BIG SPORTS, BIG PARTIES
College Size and Social Life

The size and scope of your college or university should fit your personal profile. This chapter looks at the advantages and disadvantages of size and social life, and concludes with an important factor too many people miss when looking at colleges.

Large Versus Small

Size is cited as a factor in almost every conversation I have with students (or parents) about what they're looking for in a college or why they chose one. It's often one of the first criteria students use when screening colleges, and it tends to spark instant emotion.

Some students reflexively want to go big after attending a small high school, while others are scared of getting lost in a large university. These are often gut reactions that can lead to fixation, because it's too early in the process to narrow a search based on feelings.

Instead, zoom out to view the positives and negatives objectively. Look at how they relate to the education you need and the type of learner you are, along with the transferable skills and mental habits you need to develop.

If You Go Big

Big universities have a wide range of courses and majors along with exceptional facilities. However, courses can sometimes be difficult to get into and that can delay graduation, especially if you switch majors. You might need to be persistent and plan ahead to get into courses or take a few classes online to avoid delaying graduation.

None of this is ideal, but there can be potential benefits. Learning to take initiative, plan in advance, and push through administrative obstacles can develop transferable skills and strong mental habits. Persistence, planning, and initiative might also be necessary with career services, student activities, or finding academic support. All of that can be good, bad, or indifferent, depending on your needs.

A large university might be a good match if you learn better in larger classes or have a more independent learning style. Big universities can have professors with big reputations, but you'll probably share their time with graduate students and the professors' research agendas, so graduate assistants are likely to teach some of your classes.

If You Go Small

Small colleges tend to flourish by counterprogramming a large university experience. Their size and scope can result in a stronger sense of community. Professors teach all classes at most small colleges. Class sizes tend to be smaller, too. That means you can get to know your professors. In fact, that's why many of them choose to teach in small colleges.

The range of courses might be smaller than big universities, but enrolling in courses tends to be easier. They also have fewer majors from which to choose, but a lot of small colleges allow students to design their own major. Academic advising, academic support, and career services are usually more accessible and personalized.

Many small colleges have exceptional facilities, too, and like universities, they provide research opportunities for students. While big universities have more alumni for job networking, small colleges can have a core group who are very loyal to their school and willing to help fellow alums. There may be fewer activities, but with fewer students, there can be a greater chance to participate.

On the other hand, a small college might feel limiting, especially after the first two years. This could mean extra effort to get off campus and add variety to your activities, but that can be a good thing to learn. You can also study abroad at a large university to balance the small school experience. While small colleges make a greater effort to personalize a student's time on campus, it can still feel like you're in a bubble and missing the challenges of a large university.

Regardless of size, you're likely to spend most of your time with a small group of friends, and you'll struggle to imagine going to any other college—big or small—without them.

Do Your Homework

The decision on school size should come down to what you need, which takes time to figure out. It's important to consider size carefully. In time, students with knee-jerk reactions to go big might decide going small is best for them. Of course, the opposite can happen, too.

Finally, there are colleges/universities with mid-size enrollments. These appeal to students who want to split the difference for the best of both worlds. Do your homework on these. Just because a college seems to offer the advantages of both doesn't make it true.

Sports and Parties in Twenty Years

Too many students overweight the importance of a fun social scene or sporting events in their college decisions, including Greek life (fraternities and sororities). It's not uncommon to hear someone say they want a university with big sports events, while big parties are just as desirable for some students, even if it's unspoken.

A search based on what really matters is likely to result in the realization that there's more to college than sports and parties. Again, it's okay to like these elements, but they should be used as tiebreakers, when your highest priorities are equal.

That said—and I'm sorry for the need to be blunt—if you still want to use sports and parties as major decision points, then it's time to rethink your priorities.

- Do you really want big sports or big parties near the top of your list when figuring out where to spend the huge amount of time and money college requires?

- In twenty years, will you regret missing out on sporting events and parties more than finding the best place to maximize your potential?

It's possible to have both, as long as you avoid rationalizations. Besides, small colleges can have exciting sporting events and parties, too.

The big sports/big party scene also cuts both ways. It can attract students *and* scare others away. So it's important not to let them turn you off from a large university that might be your best option.

Finally, there's nothing wrong with joining a fraternity or sorority, if there is one that fits within your broader plan for a foundational experience, which depends on your personal profile and the nature of the particular fraternity/sorority.

Fraternity/sorority activities should not consume all of your time outside of classes. Be careful. When recruitment begins, look at the expectations for your time, along with the safety record on hazing rituals and other similar activities. Innocent, fun rituals are one thing, but houses that cross the line into *hardcore*, prove-you-are-worthy-type stuff are not worth it.

Avoid This Trap

We've touched on the human tendency to overestimate our abilities, which comes from anticipating success. You will succeed in college, but there will be ups and downs. Unfortunately, some students look past the downs when exploring colleges.

Avoid this trap.

Find a place—big or small—where you'll be comfortable making mistakes, dealing with unexpected challenges, and fulfilling your potential. Make sure the environment and support systems (health, counseling, academic support, etc.) you *might* need are there. You don't want a school that will hammer you over mistakes, or one that will coddle you. Either scenario can slow your development.

There are advantages and disadvantages to any college size, so weigh them carefully against what you need to excel.

Chapter 25

NEITHER GANDHI NOR MOTHER TERESA

Applications

This chapter introduces a simple concept to eliminate anxiety over college admissions, along with advice on applications, including the option for early decision. Some of what follows might stir up disagreement, and that's okay. The perspective you take on applications is up to you.

When high school seniors send in applications and are left to sweat over the colleges' decisions, it prompts a yearly round of articles and blog posts on how to deal with the stress and anxiety. While the advice is well intended, most of it is recycled and does nothing to eliminate pressure, since it comes too late in the admissions cycle. And it usually fails to clarify what college acceptance signals—potential and opportunity—the perspective covered in Chapter 1.

Scarcity and Eliminating High Stakes

Colleges and universities have a limited number of places for students, which means scarcity and competition are built into the system. So stress and anxiety are assumed by too many people to be unavoidable, but that raises important questions:

- What if you don't buy into scarcity?
- What if you turn the tables on competition?

There are many strong colleges and universities where you can build a foundational life experience—more than most people realize.

Instead of being swept up by scarcity, ignore it. Turn the tables and make colleges compete for *your* application, regardless of acceptance rates.

How does that eliminate stress?

If you put in the work to know that it's possible to have a foundational experience wherever you apply, there is no need for angst over any admissions decisions. What's the point if *wherever* you end up can provide what you need? All this takes is the extra effort to develop a plan for each college to which you apply. I'll explain how in the next section.

Applications

Do not misrepresent yourself in any college application. Be genuine. Admissions officers look for students who best match their institutions. They know the tricks and will usually spot falsehoods. Besides, if your best effort ends up with a decline, then this college is *not* your best fit.

Some people will always manage to get through highly selective committees with tricked up applications. But doing that only puts them at risk of attending a college that won't serve them as well as their best fit. Some parents pay for an independent college counselor to get all of the bells and whistles into their child's applications, which means some of these parents are actually paying to find the wrong fit!

Good college admissions officers know you aren't the second coming of Mother Teresa or Mahatma Gandhi. It's also safe to say neither Gandhi nor Mother Teresa would be anything but genuine in their applications.

As for independent counselors, if you need one and can afford it, there's nothing wrong with getting help. But skip the tricks. Make sure the counselor is helping to find your best school, based on what you need to fulfill your potential. And if you come across a counselor who *promises* to get you into highly selective institutions, run for the hills.

Application Options

Most students submit applications in the regular admissions cycle. These are usually due by early January with notifications sent around mid-March to early April. Students generally have until May 1—sometimes called National College Decision Day—to let colleges know if they want to attend.

Colleges and universities also offer different admissions options that let students learn their status sooner. These include early decision, early action, and rolling admissions.

Early Decision

Early Decision applications are due mostly around the first two weeks of November and notifications arrive around mid-December. Financial aid applications must be submitted earlier, too, and the last chance for Early Decision applicants to take the SAT/ACT comes early as well.

Early Decision applications also carry *a binding commitment* that, if accepted, students will attend this college/university. That limits you to one early decision application.

I'm not a fan of Early Decision, unless you're an athlete or applying for a particular program that comes with a significant scholarship award. Aside from those cases, there's no compelling need to make a firm commitment this early in the process.

The great temptation and unfortunate reality behind Early Decision is that acceptance rates are higher, which means students with competitive applications have a better chance for acceptance than they would in the regular pool, particularly at highly selective institutions. Yet, Early Decision risks traps like fixation, jumping the process, and confirmation bias through impatience, decision fatigue, or rationalizing other reasons.

If you go for Early Decision, a proper search is still required to determine your number-one choice. I'll cover these steps in the next section. Athletes should aim to find the right college first, not a team/coach. Playing careers can end quickly through injury or other factors, so be certain the college or university you attend is the right place.

By sending your application, you're pushing up the college decision to November, instead of the following April/May. *A lot can happen in these months.* Personal development can accelerate rapidly at this stage in your life. And, after you're enrolled, Early Decision is not a guarantee you'll do better than those admitted in the regular cycle.

Early Action

Colleges and universities with Early Action allow students to apply early and find out if they're accepted *without* a binding commitment to attend. Unlike Early Decision, you can apply elsewhere and don't need to let the colleges know your final decision until the same time as students accepted through the regular process.

Early Action dates tend to mirror those for Early Decision, but there is variety, so stay on top of application deadlines and when notifications will be sent. A few colleges place restrictions on Early Action, so always check policies before applying.

Early Action is a viable option, if you avoid decision traps.

Rolling Admissions

Rolling Admissions sees colleges and universities offer an open window for applications, sometimes for six months or more. Students are usually notified in about four to six weeks. If admitted through rolling admissions, accepted students can decide to enroll at any point, with a final deadline that usually coincides with the regular cycle at other colleges. The chances of acceptance tend to be greater for applications sent earlier in a rolling admissions window, so it can be a big mistake to think of this as a last-minute back-up plan.

Be it Early Decision, Early Action, or Rolling Admissions, never feel pressure to make a decision until you're absolutely sure.

Chapter 26

WHAT'S YOUR FLAVOR?
College and University Profiles

Let's look at the wide range of degree-granting, four-year colleges and universities. This might be boring, but it's quick, contextual information you should know. Here are the college and university profiles available in American higher education.

Colleges Versus Universities

Colleges generally focus on undergraduate students pursuing bachelor's degrees (e.g., B.A., B.S.). *Universities* serve both undergraduate students and graduate students seeking bachelor's, master's, or doctoral degrees (e.g., B.A., B.S., M.A., M.S., MBA, M.Ed., PhD).

Many four-year colleges offer a few masters-level degrees. Some of these have opted to change their name, for example, from XYZ College to XYZ University. This is done largely for branding purposes, and that means not every "university" has a large enrollment or offers a wide range of graduate degrees.

Large universities are organized into divisions identified as colleges (e.g., the College of Nursing, College of the Arts, College of Business, College of Education, etc.). Many universities have established honors colleges that try to emulate liberal arts colleges within their broader university setting. While it's hard to replicate a pure liberal arts college, these are worth exploring, especially if they're a good fit financially.

Public Versus Private

Funding sources and institutional governance determine whether institutions are public or private. You don't need to worry about governance, but financing is relevant to tuition and financial aid.

Private colleges and universities generally rely on tuition and fees, donations from alumni and parents, and other private funding sources. Their endowments are essentially large savings/investment accounts from which a small amount (about 5 percent) is used every year as an additional revenue source. That's how wealthy schools offer generous financial aid packages.

Public colleges and universities get funding from the same sources as the privates, but they also receive support from their state governments. State support has declined over the past several decades but remains a significant funding source. This government support is why tuition is lower for in-state students.

Whether public or private, additional revenue sources allow institutions to operate on a higher cost-per-student basis than the revenue they collect from students' tuition and fees. That's why the actual per-student cost to a college or university is almost always greater than even the sticker price for full paying students.

Special Mission Institutions

There are colleges and universities with a special mission or other unique qualities: arts colleges, work colleges, engineering colleges, conservatories, single-gender colleges, and religious colleges. Work colleges offer reduced tuition in exchange for students working across the college's operations, which reduces operating costs. More information on these can be found at *www.workcolleges.org*.

There are still a few single-gender, private colleges that enroll only women or only men. There are many religiously affiliated colleges and universities, but those that infuse religion into their students' day-to-day lives fall into a specialty category.

Special mission colleges include Appalachian, Historically Black Colleges and Universities (HBCU), and Hispanic-Serving Institutions (HSI). Other colleges have highly specialized missions. For example, Landmark College in Vermont serves students with diagnosed learning difficulties, while Gallaudet University in Washington, D.C., serves students who are deaf or hard of hearing.

Community Colleges

Community colleges have developed considerably over the past several decades and can provide a compelling value to students. Some have begun to offer a few four-year degrees, however, most stick with the traditional two-year associate degrees and other certifications, which can qualify their recipients for rewarding careers.

Students can also transfer from community colleges to four-year institutions and earn a bachelor's degree. That usually involves meeting a number of general education requirements before transferring. Tuition is generally much lower at community colleges, so they can offer a viable and affordable option, as you'll see in the next chapter.

For-Profit Colleges and Universities

These are *companies* with "college" or "university" in their names. They are accredited to offer a range of degrees, but unlike their non-profit counterparts, these organizations are in business to profit from their operations. Generally, they prepare students for a specific career.

While I have no direct experience with these companies, I still urge caution. As you saw in Chapter 2, they tend to have much lower graduation rates than nonprofit colleges and universities. And depending on the company, students might find difficulty transferring credits.

Chapter 27

MONEY DOESN'T HAVE FEELINGS
College Costs/Affordability

This chapter deals with financial aid and other considerations for the cost of college. I'm not a financial expert and don't pretend to be one, so you can judge the value of what we cover. If there's a broader point to everything in this chapter, it's to *be careful*. The national crisis in student loan debt means too many students struggle to afford college.

There are very fortunate students whose parents or grandparents can afford the full cost of any college. If you're one of them, I hope you're deeply grateful, but that good fortune is not an excuse to skip this chapter. There are still issues you might need to consider, if not for college, then graduate school and beyond.

The High School Versus College Payoff

Chapter 23 covered why average earnings projections based on majors/jobs/careers aren't always reliable at the individual level. What you can count on, though, is the projected difference in earnings for college graduates versus high school graduates.

The Pew Research Center found the gap between *average yearly earnings* for high school graduates and college graduates (between ages of 25 and 32) is $17,500[1], and the gap has been increasing since

---

1   "The Rising Cost of Not Going to College," Pew Research Center, February 11, 2014, *http://www.pewsocialtrends.org/2014/02/11/the-rising-cost-of-not-going-to-college/*.

1965. This figure is based on average earnings, so there will be some variation, but that's a huge difference.

The wage gap doesn't fully explain why college costs so much, yet it certainly shows why people are willing to pay for rising college costs.

While it's safe to say a college graduate is highly likely to earn more than a high school graduate, it's impossible to predict someone's career earnings over thirty or more years. There are a ton of personal variables in how life plays out. Throw in all of the possible economic scenarios, including the tech revolution, and everyone is left with a leap of faith.

None of this is meant to discourage, but rather to explain why you should manage expectations with realistic earnings estimates. For example, if your heart is set on becoming a doctor or lawyer, your career earnings can still vary in relation to the average lawyer or doctor. It's important to avoid overestimating what you'll earn. Go for it. Absolutely. Just be careful with financial expectations, which should include the possibility that you'll switch to a lower paying profession.

All Future Costs

Graduate school is expensive. Although you might not go beyond an undergraduate degree, you're still too young to rule it out. If you think there's even a slight possibility that you'll go for an advanced degree, then consider those costs now.

Graduate school can be viewed as a financial transaction, because it is largely about professional advancement/training. Feel free to use a cost/benefit perspective—X to Y to Z. Career earnings for a doctor, lawyer, or other highly paid professions should account for the cost of law school, or medical school. The same goes for any other graduate degree necessary to excel in a profession. As always, do the research before making graduate school decisions.

Overpaying for an undergraduate degree will impact your ability to pay for graduate school or other types of professional training. Students stuck with heavy loans from an undergraduate degree should probably take time to pay off some debt before taking on more loans for graduate school.

Yet, there are students who opt for a risky route by going straight to graduate school and increasing their debt. Anyone doing that better know their career path without question. Delaying payments, increasing debt, *and* making a major career decision is a very high-stakes move, especially with limited (if any) work experience in the field.

Financial Aid

Financial aid is complicated, which is unfortunate, because it is critical to most students' ability to pay for college. We covered additional revenue sources in the last chapter, and why the per-student cost for almost any college or university is more than the listed "sticker price" for tuition and fees. In other words, even full-paying students have a built-in discount.

The amount of aid students receive varies from college to college, so you can't determine the actual cost without the financial aid package from a college that accepts you. Remember what was noted in the questions and answers for Section One: if you reject possible colleges because you *assume* they are unaffordable, that cuts down your options and essentially underthinks your decision.

Private colleges generally have high sticker prices, but they regularly offer reduced tuition based on a student's financial need. It's worth exploring private options for hidden value. If the course availability at a private means you can finish in four years versus five or more at a public institution, then the *overall cost* could be less, or close the price gap considerably on what might be a better experience.

Initially, it's best to keep your options open through a balance of public and private possibilities, both in and out of state.

Start the financial aid process early. All students who need aid must apply for it. This process is separate from admissions applications, with more forms and deadlines. *Do not wait until a college or university accepts you to apply for financial aid.* "Need-Blind" colleges and universities do not factor financial aid into their admissions decisions.

A good college counselor can help, as should the college and universities that interest you. But *you need to take the initiative*, and that starts with learning the basics for financial aid.

Financial Aid Resources

You can find strong information in books and websites for learning the ins and outs of financial aid:

- The College Board has a website called Big Future: (*www.bigfuture.collegeboard.org*). The Pay for College tab includes a link to Financial Aid 101.

- Despite my skepticism for rankings, the *U.S. News* website has useful information, including College Financial Aid 101, which can be found in the Paying for College section (*https://www.usnews.com/education/best-colleges/paying-for-college/financial-aid-101*).

- Lynn O'Shaughnessy's book *The College Solution* helps students find the right school at the right price.[2]

- FinAid (*www.finaid.org*) is filled with information about financial aid.

- Sallie Mae (*www.salliemae.com*) provides information on student loans and financial aid.

---

2   Lynn O'Shaughnessy, *The College Solution* (Upper Saddle River, New Jersey: Pearson Education, Inc., 2012).

Financial Aid Applications

Financial aid revolves around the following applications:

- FAFSA® (*http://fafsa.ed.gov*): Free Application for Federal Student Aid (FAFSA®) is the federal form for financial aid used by public colleges and universities. Don't miss deadlines for submitting, and taxes need to be filed before filling out the form. Although, you can get an estimate on your *expected family contribution* (EFC) at *https://studentaid. ed.gov/sa/fafsa/estimate*.

- The CSS Profile™ (*https://cssprofile.collegeboard.org*) is required by many private institutions to determine eligibility for aid. Some private colleges rely only on the FAFSA®, but many privates, including the most competitive, require the CSS Profile™.

The FAFSA® will not ask about home equity (the value of your home minus what is owed to the lender), but the CSS factors it in. There are differences in how colleges use home equity to determine a student's eligibility for aid. Ask how much home equity will be a factor, if necessary.

Financial Aid Calculators

Financial calculators are available on most college and university websites. These can be helpful because of the differences between the FAFSA® and CSS Profile™ calculations.

While results are unofficial projections, these estimates can help determine if it's worth sending an admissions application. The Big Future and FinAid sites also have them, while Lynn O'Shaughnessy has useful advice on calculators that you can find here: *http://www. thecollegesolution.com/why-you-must-use-college-net-price-calculators/*.

Negotiating Financial Aid Packages

Good students with difficult economic situations usually receive generous financial aid. It's trickier for the middle class. *What the colleges say you can afford might be different from what you think.*

These discrepancies have led a growing number of students to challenge financial aid decisions. Chapter 14 of *The College Solution* offers good advice on how to appeal an aid package. O'Shaughnessy's best recommendation is to keep emotions out of it.

There's also no need to feel embarrassed about trying to negotiate a better deal. Money doesn't have feelings. Besides, the college administrators you'll deal with are professionals. They know (or should) that offering financial aid results in a flexible pricing model, and having one leaves them open to questions about improved packages.

Temper your expectations. As a general rule, most students who challenge aid packages get only minor adjustments, if any. Yet, marginal adjustments can add up, and if legitimate misunderstandings are clarified, a more significant adjustment might be made.

Academic Scholarships/Merit Aid

Students with exceptional talents/accomplishments can qualify for merit aid at colleges and universities that offer it. These academic or merit scholarships are not based on financial need.

If you think you can earn one, look for merit aid opportunities on college websites to see if your scholastic achievements and/or extracurricular activities might qualify. Some colleges will nominate students directly from their applicant pools without students having to pursue them.

Athletic Scholarships

If you're pursuing college athletics, understand that Division III athletes do not receive athletic scholarships. Their financial support must come through need- or merit-based aid.

Beyond the major revenue producing sports, full-ride athletic scholarships are rare at the NCAA Division I and II levels. There are some trickle-down effects to athletes in other sports at schools with major football and basketball programs, but few athletes outside of these sports are on full athletic scholarships. Most Division I and II athletes receive partial scholarships that are renewed annually. Coaches tend to spread scholarship budgets across their rosters. Athletes who qualify for need-based aid can still receive athletic scholarships, but athletic aid usually offsets need-based aid.

High-end youth sports programs have become a huge business in the United States. While the benefits from participating can include life lessons, transferable skills, fitness, friendships, confidence, etc., parents who spend a lot of time, travel, and money should *not* see this as an investment that will pay off through a big money athletic scholarship.

Can it be an investment in the benefits just listed?

Yes. But a huge scholarship that effectively pays you back is scarce. (Parents: If you think your child will be that rare, 99th-percentile exception, you're not alone. And even if your child has what it takes to get the full scholarship, an injury during prime recruiting months or other unforeseen issues can wipe it out.)

Private Scholarships

Private scholarships are available throughout the country from corporations, foundations, associations, etc. These can be used at public or private institutions. The awards are considered private because they are granted separately from federal, state, or college/

university-based support. Private scholarships are pursued by students on their own initiative. There are many opportunities for students with a wide variety of attributes and circumstances.

Caution is necessary. Never pay anything to apply for a scholarship, because it's probably a scam. Scholarships with national- or state-applicant pools are highly competitive. Even local, high-dollar awards will attract serious competition.

Please don't think private scholarships can be a primary form of financial aid. Only a handful of students earn the big ones. As Lynn O' Shaughnessy puts it, "Private scholarships are the puniest source of college cash. . . . Only about 7 percent of college students receive a private scholarship, and the average award is roughly $2,500. They are often only good for one year."[3]

Finally, like athletic scholarships, private scholarships might result in a deduction from need-based financial aid.

Depending on your abilities and circumstances, private scholarships could add up to make a difference. Still, *all students should make federal, state, and institution-based aid their top priority.*

Student Loans: Money Can Work For or Against You

The student-loan crisis has grown for decades. As we've covered, it stems *partly* from overestimating future earnings based on the profession students think they want. It can also come from students and parents who don't account fully for the added cost that comes with a loan.

If you need student loans, go with a government-backed loan and try to avoid private student loans, which can have higher interest rates or stricter terms.

To understand the actual cost of college when loans are used, let's look at how money works for or against you.

---

3   Lynn O'Shaughnessy, *The College Solution* (Upper Saddle River, New Jersey: Pearson Education, Inc., 2012), 44–45.

Compounding interest is one of money's most powerful rules. Since money accrues gains and losses, compound interest can be very helpful *or* cause serious damage to your finances.

Here's what compounding can do for a $10,000 investment. To keep it simple, taxes and inflation are not factored into the example. If $10,000 is invested over ten years and earns 5 percent interest each year (less than the historical return for the stock market), it can grow considerably in value. According to the U.S. Securities and Exchange website Investor.gov, the investment would be worth $16,289 in ten years. This example shows the positive power of compounding. Each year the investment earns interest on the original $10,000 *and* the interest already paid, since the money is left in the account.

Compounding is great for investment purposes, but it works against you when borrowing too much. *Money isn't free.* When you take out a loan, you're borrowing from a bank (lender) with the promise to pay back the amount you borrow *and* an annual interest charge for using the bank's money. In other words, the bank is investing in you to provide interest payments so their money will compound, just like the $10,000 in the previous example. If you're not willing to pay the market interest rate, the bank will find someone else.

Whenever you borrow to pay for something, you should factor interest payments into the overall cost. Let's say you borrow $20,000 with the promise to pay it off monthly over ten years at a 5 percent interest rate. The bank will expect monthly payments that cover both the interest rate and chip away at the $20,000 principal amount you owe; in this case that means a monthly payment of about $212. After ten years (120 payments), the $20,000 will be paid back along with $5,440 to cover the interest payments on the loan.

So a $20,000 purchase can actually cost a lot more when you borrow money. If you miss payments, the amount of money owed goes up and the time to pay it off takes longer. Missing payments is where compounding kicks in to really work against you, sometimes severely.

If you need a student loan, *the interest you pay is an added college cost* and that should factor into your decision.

Please don't let this scare you away from debt. Most people need to use debt at various times in their lives. For example, borrowing money to buy a car allows them to get to work, which enables them to pay for the car, food, housing, health care, utilities, insurance, etc. And almost everyone needs to borrow money when they buy a house.

Again, *be careful*.

The Community College Route

An increasing number of students are choosing to spend their early college years at less expensive community colleges. They try to meet most of their general education requirements before transferring to a traditional four-year institution where they complete a major and earn their degrees.

If this idea just caused status anxiety, your résumé only needs to list the college where you complete a degree. Although, there are employers who will respect the decision to pursue a practical and cost-effective route.

One young woman I know from California decided that the University of Utah was her best option, but the out-of-state costs were too high for her. Instead of going somewhere else, she moved to Utah, enrolled in a community college, and got a job at a ski resort. After two years at the community college, she had established Utah residency and will enroll now at the university with reduced in-state tuition. She estimates this path will save at least $30,000 (and hopefully $40,000) on the total cost for her bachelor's degree. Utah also has a great new resident.

Income Share Agreements

A handful of colleges and universities have begun to offer Income Share Agreements (ISA). Instead of student loans, ISAs cover college costs in exchange for a small percentage of a graduate's future earnings. There can be caps put in place to protect high earners from paying too much.

ISAs might sound ideal to some people, but they are not widespread, and there simply isn't enough long-term data to assess the real risk to students. Until a reasonable judgment can be made on these, anyone who signs up for an ISA is pioneering this repayment approach.

My only advice, with absolute certainty, is to think it through very carefully before you commit and avoid anything that might lock you into specific professions.

Know Your Amount

Finally, anyone who doesn't know the total dollar amount or a viable range—from start to finish—for what they can *reasonably afford* to pay for college is swimming naked. This might seem obvious, but the student-debt crisis suggests too many people whiff on it. Consult a financial expert, if necessary.

Projecting college costs should include tuition, room and board (on or off campus), fees, books, travel to and from home, healthcare, social life, etc. Ask about planned increases, because the costs are likely to rise a little each year.

Always read the fine print on a financial aid package and/or the terms of a student loan. There's no need to be shy about asking questions—then ask more.

Chapter 28

GOING AWAY IS CLOSER THAN IT USED TO BE

Section Four Questions & Answers

How can I give my best effort to college classes and still have time for a foundational experience?

Balance. College is a great time to learn how to achieve it. This is where planning comes in. If you want a foundational experience, you can make it happen.

But you don't understand . . .

Actually, I do. Don't worry about "what ifs" or anything else that winds you up. Be deliberate. Plan and prioritize for what matters the most. Then, do the best you can in the time you have. Everything else will work out.

Do you really expect college students to be intentional learners, 24/7?

No. You should turn your brain off and relax or you'll go nuts. That's another reason why balance is important. The problem comes from neglecting intentional learning, which is a mental habit that takes discipline. You can think while walking around campus, doing workouts, riding a bus, or a few minutes before bed. You can also talk about it with friends. All of that will accumulate to your benefit.

You were kind of a mess in college, so when did you figure out it was important to be an intentional learner?

On a frozen lake in Minnesota.

Should I take an SAT/ACT preparation course?

Do what's best for you. Standardized tests happen at a fixed point in time. They measure a relatively narrow set of academic skills, which help predict your *current* ability for college level coursework. And an increasing number of colleges don't require standardized tests.

Good college admissions officers will put your scores in context with your high school transcript and other factors. In their eyes, a great score can help, of course. But if your grades are better than your test scores, that can still help, depending on the challenge of your high school courses and the competition within the application pool. Of course, high test scores with relatively low grades need a good explanation.

Test preparation is your decision. A reasonably priced SAT/ACT prep class is a viable option. But it's also fine to prepare on your own, take the test, and live with the result. You won't be the first or last to do that. If you don't like the result, then take a prep course or take the test again.

Does distance from home matter as much as some people think?

This might sound like Yogi Berra, but going away is closer than it used to be. Technology is shrinking the world. The distance you choose between home and college should depend on your *need* to be physically close to family and hometown friends. Of course, travel costs should be a factor, too.

Should I consider graduate school while looking at undergraduate options?

Only the financial aspects. Overpaying for an undergraduate degree will hurt your ability to pay for a graduate degree. Beyond that, focus on the best option for an undergraduate degree. There's plenty of time to figure out graduate school. You'll also need time for academic and personal development *before* you can make a great decision on graduate school.

This applies even if you decide to pursue a program that leads straight from a BA to an MA. You can start on that track, but you shouldn't feel trapped if your experience in the first few years justifies a change.

Do grades matter in college?

Yes. Grades matter for graduate school applications and employers might want to see your grade point average (GPA) when you apply for jobs soon after college. If you don't plan on graduate school, you should still give your best effort. Strive for achievement rather than box checking. Your grades will then provide accurate guidance for determining a major and potential careers.

How much does a college major really matter?

It matters. No question. However, you don't need to know your major when applying to college. Explore your interests and options in the early college years, then make a decision on the best possible major. People who think a high school senior should know exactly what major(s) to pursue are misguided, at best. Even if you're absolutely convinced of what you want to do in life, it's still a good idea to research other options in case you change your mind. Plan A should always come with Plan B and Plan C.

What if I'm already in college and thinking about transferring?

A knee-jerk decision to transfer might create more problems, and these could turn out to be worse than what you want to transfer from. Set your emotions aside. Go back to the reasons for choosing the college in the first place. If the reasons hold up, stay. Have courage in your convictions.

If your reasoning was legitimately flawed, then find good reasons to stay. Try to figure out how this college can be a better anchor for a foundational experience. If you still come up short, then start the search process for a transfer. Weigh the pros and cons of the colleges/universities you explore against each other *and* your current situation.

I'm still not certain about college, so what should I do?

Think carefully. You still need a plan for personal and professional development. If you're conflicted about going to college or need time to save money, then a gap year could help. You will need strong reasons for taking one, a good plan, and the self-discipline to see it through.

Some high school graduates need time away from formal schooling to figure out what they value most, need, and want to do in college. That can include working in a professional field as a test drive. *Do not feel ashamed if you need more time.* Instead, be proud of having the confidence and self-awareness to take a different path. Just be aware that future applications for colleges and possibly jobs will need to show how the time spent was valuable.

Your College Search and Decision

SECTION FIVE

Section Five Preview

This Section brings us to your search and decision. We'll cover the three phases of the decision triangle—Big Picture to Middle to Final—and what it takes to do this well. Before reading the chapters to come, here is the triangle introduced in Section Two.

YOUR COLLEGE SEARCH/DECISION PROCESS

BIG PICTURE PHASE
Think broadly to determine what matters the most: information, beliefs, interests, goals, values, needs, your academic and personal profiles.

MIDDLE PHASE
Evaluate a range of colleges and universities based on important criteria, and then narrow these to a manageable pool of options.

FINAL PHASE
Determine where to apply. Gather acceptances and do final cross-checks. Then, step back and decide.

Your Best College or University

Big Picture Phase

Chapter 29 explains the reasoning behind the process you are asked to follow and shows how to develop a healthy bias for your search and decision.

Chapter 30 outlines a discovery process to refine your big-picture thinking.

Chapter 31 covers how to create a preliminary plan for a foundational life experience.

Middle Phase

Chapter 32 helps develop a manageable list of possibilities.

Chapter 33 introduces criteria for evaluating the colleges/universities on your list.

Final Phase

Chapter 34 helps determine where to apply.

Chapter 35 covers the waiting period after applications are sent and the last steps for your decision.

Chapter 36 offers final thoughts.

Chapter 29

TRUST THE PROCESS
Healthy Bias and Cross-checks

Everything I've covered to this point, be it information or advice, is what you need to know. This section covers what you need to do. It's best to read the entire section first. The Appendix provides a sample evaluation template to compare and contrast colleges, along with two other templates included in this section. You will also find downloadable versions of these at *wheneagleslaunch.com*.

Lasting Value and Immediate Benefits

The importance of *why* you do something echoes throughout the book. Since a few parts of this approach might feel like ditch digging, it's essential to understand the reasons behind it.

Chapter 1 explains the difference between accomplishment and true achievement, noting that true achievers work *up to and through* results. That's what this section is about. Instead of one goal, it will help you achieve three goals:

1. Find the right college for the right reasons—a place that meets your personal, professional, and financial needs;

2. *Prepare* to have a foundational life experience in your college years; and

3. Learn how to make a professional-caliber decision.

Combined, these goals will help you capture the greatest lasting value from an important moment in your life.

And beyond the long-term value of these goals, this process brings two immediate benefits:

1. As noted in the last section, if you can have a foundational life experience at every college/university to which you apply, there will be no point in stressing over admissions decisions; and

2. The thinking you are asked to do throughout the process will serve as strong preparation for writing your personal statement and other application essays.

The first benefit might seem obvious, but don't overlook the second one. Colleges and universities are looking for the best students that fit their admissions criteria, programs, and culture. That means your essays and other written answers will need to make a strong case for why you are a great fit at each college/university where you apply.

Expected and Unexpected Challenges

Getting your head right starts with understanding *why* you are going to do something a certain way—hence the first four sections of this book. Keeping your head right starts with being mentally prepared for challenges that you know will come, and acknowledging unexpected challenges when they arise.

For example, *the college search/decision will challenge the mental habits we've covered.* Emotions will flare immediately when you look at colleges. Some of the programs, facilities, and all-around feel might blow you away, and it will be tempting to think of one or two as a "no-brainer." Yet, feelings of excitement can knock you out of alignment.

And the opposite is true.

Negative knee-jerk reactions might tempt you to reject colleges that could turn out to be a great experience. Thoughts like, "That's good enough," or "I'm just going to . . ." or "I don't have time to . . ." will be *very* tempting, but none of these get you to the level of achievement a quality search requires. Or, if you're looking at highly selective colleges, the sense of scarcity could wind you up.

Trust the process. That will avoid decision traps, smooth out ups and downs, and keep your focus on what matters the most.

You can do this, so here we go.

Developing Your Healthy Bias

Chapter 9 explains why bias is unavoidable and that decisions should be shaped around a set of healthy biases. In the case of a college search and decision, it's best to start with written answers for the following questions. Listed in order from most to least:

- What do you fear about going to college?
- What excites you about going to college?

Be honest and list everything, but also find the balance between underthinking and overthinking.

When these lists are complete, the fears and desires near the top of each one are the unhealthy biases that are most likely to drive your college decision. Except by identifying these now, you can transform your lists into a healthy set of biases.

Cross-checks

The four cross-checks below provide discipline to reshape your lists into a healthy set of biases. As you proceed, shrink the lists to what matters the most. There's no need to rush. *Versions of these cross-checks can apply to almost any major decision throughout your life.* And with experience, you'll become better and faster using cross-checks as a decision-making tool.

Take a hard look at your lists and revise them as you go.

Deflect Check

- Is anything on the list of fears deflecting for a deeper, more important fear?
- Does your list of desires include anything that's actually covering for a deep-seated fear?

Rational Check

- Are your fears justified or just winding you up?
- If any fears come true, will the consequences actually be as bad as you think?
- Are your desires based on realistic expectations?
- Are any fears or desires driven by misguided cultural cues or unhealthy competitive traits?

Long-Term Check

- Will everything on your lists matter in three to five years?
- Will they matter when you are 40 years old?

Wants and Needs Check

- Do the lists reflect important needs?
- Are needs given priority over wants?

It's okay to finish with short lists. The healthy biases that remain will shape your thinking throughout the search and decision process, *and* as you follow through on them during your college years.

Negative or unhealthy bias runs rampant when people gravitate to shortcuts. Developing healthy biases takes awareness and effort. This is the first and most important step toward properly thinking through a major decision.

Chapter 30

REFINE THE BIG PICTURE
Who You Are and What You Need

It's time to refine your Big Picture thinking. To do this well, you will need written answers to questions on a variety of topics. This part of the process is about personal discovery, and it will form a preliminary search plan. *There are no right or wrong answers,* only what's best for you. It's okay if your answers seem to be all over the place, or if there's some overlap.

Long answers are not necessary. *A sentence or two works for most, and some might need a short list.* The cross-checks from the last chapter can help you stay focused on what matters. After this step, you might have a few Big Picture elements left to resolve, but having thought big first means you'll be well ahead of the curve when entering the Middle Phase.

Interests/Values/Wants/Needs

You've probably thought about some of these questions before. Now, it's time to write them down:

- What do you value/need in life?
- What do you want most from college?
- What do you need most from college?
- What academic subjects interest you?
- What activities interest you?
- What other subjects and activities do you need to explore?

- What subjects and activities do you hate? Why? Do you need to hate them?

Your Academic Profile

No one can build strengths or improve weaknesses without identifying them. If you struggle answering some of the following questions, ask your teachers and college counselor for their opinion.

- What are your strongest and weakest academic subjects?

- Do your grades represent a best effort across all subjects? If not, which fall short and why? What do you need in a college to max your effort?

- If you are near the top of your high school class, can you handle being in the bottom fifty percent of your college class? If not, why? If yes, how?

- Do you need a competitive or more supportive environment to excel in college? Or, a little of both?

- Do you perform better in small classes with more attention from teachers or larger classes with less attention?

- How well do you do with project-oriented learning? What about self-directed/independent learning?

Your Transferable Skills Profile

Chapter 22 provides a list of transferable skills. After reviewing them, write the answers to these questions:

- What are your strongest and weakest transferable skills?

- Which academic subjects can help build your strengths and improve weaknesses?

- What activities do you need (classes, jobs, internships, on- and off-campus activities, etc.) to advance your transferable skill set?

Possible Major(s)

There's no need to decide on a major now; however, you should think about possibilities. Based on your current academic and career interests:

- What three or more majors do potential colleges need to offer? (It's okay if these majors reflect different interests.)
- What are your thoughts on career-oriented majors versus liberal arts majors? (Re-reading that part of Chapter 22 should help.)

Preserve options for now. Don't worry if you're stumped on possible majors or seem interested in too many.

College Size, Social Life, and Diversity

We covered the pros and cons of college size in Chapter 24. Based on some of your previous answers in this section, think about an ideal college size as you answer these questions:

- Do you need a big or small environment? Why?
- Can you be open to both? If so, why?
- Is your ideal social life big, small, or in between?
- What level of diversity do you need? (Think in terms of cultural/ethnic, religious, intellectual, and political diversity.)

Remember that *why* matters twice, so write strong answers. These will be tested in your college years.

Distance, Location, and Setting

What you determine for distance, location, and campus setting will either open or narrow your options.

- Do you need to be close to home?

- Will travel costs be an issue?
- Is there a region of the country you need to be in? If so, why?
- Do you want an urban, rural, or suburban campus setting? Why?

The cross-checks from the previous chapter should be helpful with these answers, too.

Affordability

The resources listed in Chapter 27 can help answer the following questions. If you have trouble, consult your college counselor or a financial adviser.

- What is your FAFSA® expected family contribution (EFC)?
- What can you afford to spend for a bachelor's degree *without* debt?
- If necessary, what level of debt can you *reasonably* afford for an undergraduate degree? (Potential graduate school costs should be a factor.)
- Will you need to work during college to help with expenses?
- Are you considering professions that could make it difficult to pay off student loans? If not, is it *possible* you could still end up in a lower paying profession?

Other Issues

This book is written for a broad audience, which makes it impossible to address all individual needs. If you have any big-picture issues not addressed by the categories I've outlined, then add them here.

When the answers to the questions posed in this chapter represent your best effort, move on. If not, stick with it until they do.

Chapter 31

YOUR FOUNDATIONAL EXPERIENCE
A Preliminary Plan

Since where you go to college will anchor a foundational life experience, you can't finalize a plan until you know where you're going. *But if you want to find the best colleges or universities to anchor your experience, you have to know what to look for.*

This chapter helps identify more specific elements and sketch out a preliminary plan for a foundational experience. Nothing is set in stone. You can always revise your thoughts later, if strong reasons arise.

Matching a Foundational Experience to Your Values and Interests

Here is the list from Chapter 21 of the possible components to build a foundational experience in your college years:

- courses (core curriculum for graduation, requirements for a major, and electives);
- service learning/community service;
- student activities;
- study abroad/school-sponsored trips;
- research with a professor;
- a capstone experience (a culminating project that integrates classroom learning with outside experiences);

- a gap year;
- athletics (varsity, club, or recreational);
- independent living (away from home);
- off-campus jobs while enrolled in classes;
- summer jobs/professional internships; and
- work/study on-campus jobs.

It's important to think about how these components can be part of a plan. And remember, you don't have to do everything.

Before dealing with the full list, I need to explain the gap year option.

Considerations for a Gap Year

A gap year is probably the biggest decision on the list. It can alter when you apply to college, unless you decide to defer enrollment after acceptance.

The time and opportunity a gap year can provide means nobody should blow off the idea. It's best to review what's covered on gap years in Chapter 21. Then, answer these questions:

- Do you need extra time for maturity, reflection, or self-discovery? Why?
- Can you develop a strong plan for a full year?
- When is the best time for *you* to take a gap year—before, during, or after college?
- Based on your profiles (academic, mental habits, transferable skills), what would you aim to develop during a gap year? How?
- Is a gap year necessary to earn money? Realistically, how much could you save?

There's a lot to consider here. Find the best advice.

Back to the full list.

Your List of Components

The final step in the Big Picture Phase is developing your list of components from those cited earlier. This is just a starting point to help screen potential colleges and it will be used later to develop a specific plan for each college on your eventual shortlist.

Write answers to the following:

- What do you need to accelerate your development (building on strengths and improving weaknesses)?
- Which elements match your values and interests?
- What elements do you need to learn more about?

Include a reason why each component makes the list. And since mental habits develop through everything you do, this list revolves mostly around education and developing transferable skills.

If you're stuck, put down thoughts to explain why you're conflicted. Add or drop elements as you learn more about colleges and yourself.

Remember that less can be more, so run your race. For example, outside of classes, it's better to do two things really well than spread your efforts across four or five activities. Most graduate schools and employers will not judge the amount of activities you stack up in college. A balanced approach aimed at maximizing your personal and professional potential will provide what's necessary for job or graduate school applications.

Flexible, Simple, and Obvious

Your plan should be flexible, so that it can evolve, if necessary, as you proceed through college. That allows you to incorporate the best advice you receive while in college. For example, if becoming a doctor turns out to be the best path, then your plan will need reshaping to account for pre-med courses and other activities your advisors recommend to bolster medical school applications.

Just be sure that in pursuit of a such a big goal, you don't neglect other aspects of your development. The best doctors have effective mental habits and strong transferable skills. It's often what sets them apart from average doctors. The same can be said of many other professions.

Finally, *it's okay if your list is filled with simple and obvious elements.* These combine for an effective experience, as long as they meet your needs and carry realistic expectations.

When this list is complete, along with all of the other thinking in the Big Picture Phase, you'll be ready for the Middle Phase, armed with a strong understanding of what to look for in a college or university.

Chapter 32

THE MIDDLE PHASE

A Manageable List of Possibilities

The Middle Phase sees you explore possibilities. This chapter covers guidelines to sort through *potential* colleges and universities. It finishes with three filters to narrow your search.

Good college counselors are invaluable at this stage. They can provide resources, help assess academic fit, and answer questions on financial aid/affordability. If your counselor provides a list of colleges to explore, it should be tailored to your needs, and you should still explore beyond this list.

Be open to possibilities.

Some of what you see *might* justify rethinking your goals. As you explore broadly and learn about new possibilities/needs, it's okay to revise some of your Big Picture thinking, but only if the changes can pass through the cross-checks in Chapter 29.

Sources of Information

A proper college search needs sources of information to screen for institutions. Three possibilities include:

- The College Board's Big Future website (*https://bigfuture. collegeboard.org*);

- College Navigator (*http://nces.ed.gov/collegenavigator/*), which offers the latest government data from the National Center for Education Statistics (NCES); and

- Niche (*https://www.niche.com*).

These offer effective search tools for narrowing possibilities to a manageable level.

Additional information and more in-depth profiles can be found through online college guides, such as *Peterson's* (*www.petersons. com*), *The Princeton Review* (*www.princetonreview.com*), and *U.S. News & World Report* (*www.usnews.com/best-colleges*).

Printed annual guides are also available, including *Barron's Profiles of American Colleges, Fiske Guide to Colleges,* and *The Ultimate Guide to America's Best Colleges.*

The First Three Filters

There are three filters to help identify possible options: 1) *affordability*, 2) *academic fit*, and 3) *location and setting*. College costs and academic fit must be primary factors in your decision. Location and setting are usually not as important, but they are effective for initial screening.

Affordability

To screen accurately for possibilities, you have to know what you are able/willing to pay. If you're certain, beyond any doubt, you can't afford a particular college, there's no point in exploring it further. The considerations covered on affordability in Chapter 27 should help.

Look past a college's "sticker price." College Navigator (*http:// nces.ed.gov/collegenavigator/*) and Niche (*https://www.niche.com/colleges/search/best-colleges/*) are helpful here. Both provide information on actual costs for a range of family incomes, which can be used to determine *ballpark estimates* for the cost of colleges and universities that interest you.

Niche reports net price as the average cost for students after financial aid, grants, and scholarships (as reported by the college). For example, a private liberal arts college in the Northeast with a sticker price for all costs that is over $72,000 per year can have a much different actual cost, depending on your financial need. Niche lists the *average net price* in family income ranges for this particular college as follows:

Family Income	Actual Cost Per Year
Less than $30,000	$5,141
$30,000 - $48,000	$9,505
$49,000 - $75,000	$11,186
$76,000 - $110,000	$18,577
Over $110,000	$39,398

Net price also applies to state universities. Here's an example of the average cost by income range for a flagship state university in the upper Midwest:

Family Income	Actual Cost Per Year
Less than $30,000	$7,225
$30,000 - $48,000	$9,964
$49,000 - $75,000	$17,088
$76,000 - $110,000	$22,148
Over $110,000	$24,229

These are averages. Actual costs can't be known without financial aid offers from the colleges/universities that accept you.

College Navigator's institutional profiles have a "Net Price" tab for each college and another tab with estimated expenses for full-time undergraduate students. Costs are broken down by tuition, housing options, etc. In-state and out-of-state costs are presented, too. *Note the percentage increases on the far right of the screen.*

All of this information should help project costs over a four- to six-year window. There's more to determining aid than annual income, and merit aid can't be predicted. But this information provides a good cost estimate, based on the income level you will submit in financial aid applications.

Initial Academic Fit

Academic fit is *not* a pure numbers game, but SAT/ACT scores, grade point averages (GPA), and high school class rankings still factor heavily as an initial screen for most admissions decisions. Colleges report statistics annually to help applicants understand the profile of student they generally accept. Test-optional colleges and universities don't require scores, but they do report a range of test scores for admitted students who chose to submit scores with their applications.

GPAs and class rankings can be imperfect measures because high schools vary across the country. It's impossible to make an apples-to-apples comparison of schools based on student quality, course difficulty, etc. For example, a student with a 3.8 GPA and a high class ranking at one high school could end up with a 3.5 GPA and a lesser class ranking at another high school.

Let's look at how to think through an initial screen for academic fit.

SAT/ACT Range

Test scores for the most recent entering class are available from almost every college or university.

When looking at scores, I prefer to think of quartiles. You should be able to find the 75–25 percent quartiles for the colleges you explore. For example, combined SAT scores might be presented as 1009–1175. This means that 75 percent of incoming students scored 1009 or better on the SAT, while the top 25 percent scored 1175 or higher.

If your scores fall between a college's 75–25 percent quartiles, then it's *likely* to be an academic fit. If your scores fall just below the top 75 percent (below 1009 in this example), the college could still be a fit, but you might have a greater academic challenge. If you're above the top 25 percent score, there's a better chance of being accepted, however, you might need a greater challenge, depending on your profile and other factors.

If your test scores are well above the top 25 percent, then you should probably look for a better academic match. The exception would be if the college is a tremendous fit in nonacademic ways, or you want to attend for a special program that comes with merit aid or enhanced academic programming

Test score data is presented in The College Board's Big Future website (*www.bigfuture.collegeboard.org*). For any college profile, click on the *Applying* tab, then scroll down and click on the *SAT & ACT Scores* tab to find the percentage of students accepted in a number of ranges.

I created the following profiles of ACT and SAT data to represent what you will find on the Big Future site. Under the ACT tab you'll find scores listed as follows:

ACT Composite   23–29

This represents the top 75–25 percent range. Scroll down and you also find a useful set of percentages tied to ranges of first-year student test scores, as follows:

30–36	25%
24–29	51%
18–23	23%
12–17	1%
6–11	
Below 6	

Under SAT scores you find the top 75–25 percent presented on the Big Future site like this:

SAT Reading and Writing	560–670
SAT Math	570–690
SAT Total	1140–1370

And like the ACT scores, you will find the percentages score for ranges as follows:

SAT Reading and Writing

700–800	8%
600–699	38%
500–599	38%
400–499	16%
300–399	
200–299	

SAT Math

700–800	8%
600–699	40%
500–599	44%
400–499	8%
300–399	
200–299	

Again, test scores are just a *general indicator* for where you fit and your chances for acceptance to a given college or university.

Grade Point Average (GPA) and High School Class Ranks

Despite GPAs and class ranks being difficult to compare across high schools, you should still cross-check your GPA and class rank with a college's admissions profile.

On the Big Future site, that can be found by clicking the "Academics & GPA" tab. If your test scores fall below the top 75 percent of a college's reported scores, but your GPA and class rank land *in the stronger end* of the admissions profile, you still might be a fit.

The "Academics & GPA" tab also provides helpful information on the high school courses each college requires.

Advanced Placement (AP) test scores matter for most students applying to highly selective institutions. The "AP" tab on the Big Future site has information on this.

Together, all of these data points help to estimate your academic fit and chances for admissions. *Most admissions decisions favor students who fall within a colleges' reported data points.* Although, some students are accepted when applying for long shots.

Location and Setting

Location and campus setting (urban, rural, or suburban) are the easiest filters to apply. If you're open to a national search, skip location and focus on the setting. Don't rule out too much at this stage—only exclude regions of the country that you're certain will not work. The same goes for urban, rural, or suburban settings.

The reason you keep or toss either a region or campus setting should hold up to scrutiny. For example, looking only at colleges in the South because you "like the South" isn't enough. Think it through:

- How will the South meet your needs now and in the future?
- What are the career impacts of going to a college in the South?
- How will the South have a stronger impact on your foundational experience?

Similar questions can be asked about rural, urban, or suburban settings.

Screening by location and setting, affordability, and initial academic fit should help develop a list of about twelve to fifteen colleges or universities. This is a good working number for narrowing down to your best options.

Balance Your Chances

Finally, you must balance your chances for admission by creating categories for the following list of possibilities:

- PROBABLES are colleges/universities that you can afford and are *highly likely* to accept you. There are hidden gems in this category. Do not take it lightly. (Many college counselors now refer to this category as "foundation schools" rather than "safety schools," which was a demeaning term.)
- REASONABLES offer *a decent chance* for acceptance *and* a financial aid package that will fit your goal.
- LONG SHOTS are the schools where acceptance is a reach *or* the amount of financial aid you'll receive is uncertain, relative to the sticker price.

In addition to academic fit and affordability, the institution's *acceptance rate* should be a key factor in determining where colleges land in these categories. You can find this from the data sources mentioned earlier.

Identify an equal number of Probables and Reasonables. Long Shots are optional.

Chapter 33

EFFECTIVE COLLEGE EVALUATIONS
The Criteria

E valuation is the next step —*when the colleges compete for your application*— as you compare and contrast how well they meet your needs. Try to keep the following four words in mind throughout your evaluations: **Profile** (your strengths and weaknesses), **place** (where you can excel), **price** (what you can afford), and **growth** (fulfilling your potential).

Don't be shy about asking questions. The way a college responds will tell you something. And if they don't respond, that says a lot, too. Remember, the best colleges want to be tested.

Effective *evaluation takes discipline*. Avoid jumping the process by completing an evaluation for each college or university on your list. Many of the reasons why some of these will fall short can help you determine why others are a strong fit.

Effective *evaluation also takes practice*. The quality of your evaluations will improve, along with the time it takes to complete them. After finishing the first three, set them aside. These are the ones on which you learn to evaluate. The experience gained from evaluating the full list means that it's only fair to give the first three a more experienced look to revise your original evaluations after you finish the others.

Evaluation Criteria

Colleges and universities have sophisticated marketing efforts built around terrific websites, beautiful campuses, fancy facilities, etc. And they know how to highlight what appeals to the most prospective students, which is often driven by the many students who make surface-level decisions.

If you've read this far, you're too sharp to fall for the marketing sizzle.

Aim for a professional approach to your evaluations. This requires an evaluation template that uses the same criteria to determine how well a college/university meets your needs (a sample can be found in the Appendix). This approach ensures discipline and makes it easy to compare and contrast the colleges on your list.

Each criterion should be rated with a 1 through 5, with 5 being best. Below you will find questions to help determine a rating for each. These should be followed with comments to justify the rating.

Let's look at the criteria that should factor into your evaluations.

There are a bunch of questions listed for most of the criteria, and not all of these will apply to you. Use your judgment on the questions that should be considered in your rating.

Size, Location, and Setting

Evaluate each institution, in relation to your needs, based on the location, campus setting (urban, suburban, rural) and size, with notes about the positives, negatives, and trade-offs in your comments.

Affordability

Data from the earlier screen for affordability can be reused here, along with additional information. Consider the following:

- What is the estimated total cost from day one to graduation? (Projected increases should be incorporated.)

- Are work/study options available?
- What is the average student loan debt upon graduation?
- Are merit scholarships awarded? Do you have a chance to qualify?

This rating is *temporary* until you receive official financial aid offers.

Academic Fit

Rating academic fit should include data from the initial screen (SAT/ACT range, GPA, and high school class rank), along with a comparative look at graduation rates (four-year and six-year), and retention rates (percentage of students returning after the first year).

Beyond the data, list three majors you might pursue, and feel free to add a few more. These should cover a range of possibilities. For example, chemistry, atmospheric chemistry, and meteorology won't work. There should be more variety in your choices.

Quality of teaching and class size influence the learning environment:

- Is there a mix of learning options through the traditional classroom, technology, and experiential/hands-on projects?
- What are the student-to-faculty ratio and average class size?
- Do professors teach all classes? If not, how much do they rely on graduate teaching assistants?
- Does high-course demand push students to take online courses?

Graduation requirements and elective options should be considered:

- Would the general education requirements for graduation (core curriculum) expose you to important areas beyond a major?
- How many elective courses (beyond requirements) could you take, and which ones interest you?

- Is there an introductory course/program to help with the transition to college level work?
- Can you identify courses/programs that would advance important transferable skills?
- Do any special programs or unique features interest you?
- Are there study abroad options that interest you? Would these delay graduation?

Academic advising and other support services are equally important.

- Would the advice you need be available?
- How often can you meet with your advisor?
- Is general academic support or help with specific classes readily available?
- Is academic advice linked with career advice?

Career Services

The career services office plays a key role in any foundational experience. Most colleges and universities claim a strong placement record for jobs and graduate school. Look beyond these to learn how each college can meet *your* needs/plans. Consider the following:

- When can students start working with career counselors?
- What is the job placement record *beyond* finance, law, medicine, and consulting? (Is there a culture within the college that pushes a high percentage of graduates into these fields?)
- How will the office help you find internships?
- Does the office offer personal assessments to identify interests and strengths/weaknesses for professions?
- How much of the office's resources are available after graduation?

- How strong is the alumni network? How willing are alumni to help students?

Student Services and Activities

These are important for any foundational experience.

- Is there a strong orientation program to help students transition to college life?
- Are student support services, like health and wellness, readily available?
- Are there opportunities for healthy social interactions? Do a lot of students go home or away on weekends?
- What percentage of students live off campus?
- Is there a range of activities? Which ones would advance your mental habits and transferable skills?
- Does the campus layout facilitate a balance between classes and student activities?
- Are you comfortable with campus safety measures?

Size, Location, and Setting

Evaluate each institution based on the location, campus setting (urban, suburban, rural) and size, with notes about the positives, negatives, and trade-offs in your comments.

Other Factors

If any factors unique to you came up in the Big Picture phase, include them in your evaluations, either within the existing criteria or as a separate element with a 1 through 5 rating.

Tiebreakers

Tiebreakers should be assessed as the final criteria. These include quality of housing options, campus beauty, facilities, amenities, food, etc. Be sure to keep these in perspective. If all other criteria are close, then these can be the deciding factor.

Campus Visits

Visits are *not* one of the criteria for the evaluation template. Instead, they play a key role *across* the evaluation. There's no rule on how many colleges to visit. Try for a reasonable number, if possible.

Visits should be about gathering information to make an informed decision. Imagine living and learning on each campus day after day, month after month. Walk around after a tour. Absorb what you see and hear to get a feel for each place.

Find answers to any questions that arise during a visit, and here are some other questions to consider:

- Does the visit confirm your evaluation? If not, why?
- If you visit before the evaluation stage, what do you see that needs to be confirmed when evaluating the college?
- Does what you see or hear fit with what you value and need?
- Are the negatives knee-jerk reactions you can overcome?
- Will the positives hold up over four to six years?
- Will you feel comfortable (not coddled) applying the habits of mind for a foundational experience?

Keep your eyes and ears open. Avoid quick, walk-away visits, even if you think there's no way the college is right for you. You could be having an emotional reaction. And places that don't work for you will lead to a greater appreciation for the ones that do.

When the evaluations are complete and represent your best effort, it's time for the Final phase of your search.

Chapter 34

THE FINAL PHASE
Your Applications

The Final Phase determines where to send applications, followed by a waiting period, and then a big decision on where to go. Since the scarcity problem could rear up, let's deal with it first. Stay with me on this. The following quick story makes an important point.

Scarcity

My friend Vic grew up modestly in the shadow of a steel mill near Pittsburgh. Now a retired sportswriter, Vic wore khaki pants to work every day and still waxes poetic on their durability and fashion flexibility. He learned to keep extra khakis in his closet, which he thinks of as "jars on the shelf." As the jars thin out, and only when he sees a bargain, Vic pounces to avoid paying more for khakis later. He takes care of the future, so the future can take care of the present.

You can view college applications in a similar way.

Don't Rank Them, Shelve Them

It's time to sort—not rank—your college list. Like Vic, you need "jars on the shelf." Think of your list in terms of tiers or shelves. Each evaluation should result in a college or university being placed on the metaphorical *Top Shelf* (worthy of an application), *Middle Shelf* (a possible application), or *Bottom Shelf* (toast). Ideally, you want about six to eight on the top shelf and four or more on the middle shelf. Within each shelf, there's still no need to rank them.

These shelves should not be confused with the categories that reflect your chances for acceptance. The top shelf should have an equal number of Probables and Reasonables, while Long Shots should have strong reasons for landing there.

Your shelves should look like this:

	Probables	**Reasonables**	**Long Shots**
Top Shelf	- _____	- _____	Optional
	- _____	- _____	
	- _____	- _____	
Middle Shelf	- _____	- _____	Optional
	- _____	- _____	
	- _____	- _____	
Bottom Shelf	A list of the other colleges/universities you evaluated		

Keep searching and evaluating until you have enough Probables and Reasonables on the top and middle shelves.

Eliminate the High Stakes

The next step is to know you can have a foundational life experience at each college on the Top Shelf. If not, drop these to your Middle Shelf. This is important. By doing this well, the future can take care of the present and slam the door on high-stakes pressure, since you will know that you can have a foundational experience wherever you are accepted.

You sketched out a preliminary plan from the components of a foundational life experience in the Big Picture Phase. This becomes the starting point to develop *a specific plan for each college* on your Top Shelf. Each plan should be flexible and include the following:

Time Period	Activities	Transferable Skills Acquired	Reasons
STAGE 1 Exploration:			
Time Before College			
First Academic Year			
Summer			
Second Academic Year			
Summer			
STAGE 2 Professional Pursuit:			
Third Academic Year			
Summer			
Fourth Academic Year			
Time After College			

(This form can be found at *wheneagleslaunch.com*.)

Feel free to alter the structure *within* either stage, depending on what a college offers. If summer classes are necessary, add them. If you need a fifth academic year, add that, too. *And remember that any plan should evolve as you gather advice throughout college.*

Determining Your Applications

When you have strong, realistic plans for *no less than five* colleges/universities on your Top Shelf, including at least two in the Probables category, it's time to apply. If not, look to the middle shelf or keep searching/evaluating.

Why five or more?

Options are important, especially since financial aid packages vary. But don't go crazy with double-digit applications.

Beyond eliminating pressure, *this step is key to making the colleges compete for your applications.* Comparing and contrasting actual plans is the best way to determine where to apply. These plans will also be very helpful when it's time to make the final decision after your acceptances are in.

Finally, if your parents want to be involved in the decision, you will have evaluations *and* a specific plan for each college. That should result in informed, drama-free conversations.

Clean It Up

Before sending applications, take anything off of your social media that could send the wrong message to admissions officers. It would be naïve to assume that nobody will look at your social media presence. The same goes for potential employers—be it after college or jobs and internships you want during college.

Please don't blow off this advice. Clean it up.

Submitting Applications

It's time to turn the table and dig in as you compete for acceptances to the colleges on your application list. Each college will provide application guidelines and checklists. Go with your college counselor's guidance on applications, and follow directions precisely as provided by each college. Many use the same platform, like the Common App, but additional, college specific information is usually required.

Deadlines are important. Get these on your calendar and plan accordingly. *Aim to finish applications with a month to spare*, which allows plenty of time to deal with problems that might arise.

There are a number of online sites with helpful advice for applications, including the *Applying 101* section of The College Board's Big Future website: *https://bigfuture.collegeboard.org/get-in/applying*. *Admission Matters* is a book that offers valuable application advice in Part 3: Tackling Your Applications.[1]

At this stage, your GPA, test scores, and the activities you have participated in are clearly established, and you have no control over how strong the applications will be from other students. *But you can control who writes your recommendations and how well you write your application essays.*

Not all colleges and universities accept recommendations, though the most selective generally do. Select at least one teacher you have had in the last year or two who knows you well and has witnessed your growth in the classroom. Ideally, this teacher will have seen similar growth outside of the classroom.

The Real Game

Application essays are where the real game can be won or lost. With thousands of applicants each year, admissions committees generally use grades, test scores, recommendations, etc., to narrow down their competitive pools. Final decisions—the make or break moment—can often be made on application essays—when admissions committees hear directly from you.

Applications generally ask for a personal statement, supplemental essays, and/or other short answers. These revolve around

---

1   Sally P. Springer, Jon Reider, and Joyce Vining Morgan, *Admission Matters* (San Francisco: Jossey-Bass, 2017).

questions/essay prompts designed to explore who you are, what you value, and how you came to be the person you are today. These offer a golden opportunity to make the best possible case for why you are a great fit at each college/university to which you apply.

Mixing vague generalities with the now all-too-common virtue signaling will not serve you well. Instead, you need to make a *strong case that is specific to the college/university receiving* each application. If there is something in your grades or background that needs an explanation, your essays might be the best avenue.

This is a very important step in your process, which means you need the best possible advice, so I have to defer to the college essay experts.

Follow your college counselor's lead, if you're comfortable with that advice. If not, *Admission Matters,* the book mentioned earlier, also has strong advice on writing application essays. As a starting point, you can look at the Essays section of The College Board's Big Future website (*https://bigfuture.collegeboard.org/get-in/essays*).

My advice is to be genuine. Do not misrepresent yourself, and try to have a couple of non-family members review your essays before submitting them.

Celebrate

Take time to celebrate after sending applications. This is a major accomplishment! Enjoy the rest of high school. Don't slack off, but do have fun with friends and family. The heaviest lifting is done.

Your best effort will lead to where you need to be.

Chapter 35

MAKING THE FINAL DECISION
The Last Steps to Your Best College

This chapter covers the waiting period, admissions notifications, and the final steps to making your decision.

The Waiting Period

Students have to wait for notifications and that means two problems are inevitable. The first is an urge to know, which can drive you crazy. Parents, too. But nothing shrinks the wait, so try to remember the role patience plays in grit.

The second problem is a powerful temptation to rank the colleges/universities where you have applied. We both know what's going to happen. So for the rare individual who can resist, I'll cover the ideal reasons to avoid crowning a number one. Then, we'll face reality.

The Ideal

Even at this late stage, getting fired up over a dream college can lead to some of the decision traps covered in Section Two, or set you up for disappointment through a decline. Of course, opting for Early Decision means you will have already decided on a number-one college/university.

The reasons I don't like Early Decision mirror why you should avoid ranking colleges in the regular cycle.

1. You're still in a period of rapid personal growth. Some of your thoughts, perspectives, and even circumstances could justify a change as you wait. And without the need to make a final decision, there's no need to rank them.

2. Affordability remains a major factor. Any ranking without confirmed financial aid packages will be based on incomplete information. Besides, why spend more time on a college until you're accepted and know the cost?

The Reality

Since you are *so close* to the final step and can't resist, go ahead and rank your list. Put it on paper, but write in pencil—very lightly. Be aware of the problems fixation can bring, rely on your evaluations, and don't let your expectations get too high.

Notifications

Admissions offices will send notifications that you are accepted, declined, waitlisted, or deferred.

- ACCEPTED: You're in. Congratulations! Note the date by which you must notify the college if you want to enroll. A financial aid package and other important information will be included or sent soon.

- DECLINED: You didn't make it. Too many people see declines as negative. Here's the healthy perspective: you gave your best effort only to be declined. That means you just dodged a bad situation, because this school wasn't the right place for you.

- WAITLISTED: Welcome to limbo. The waitlist means you might be accepted later, if enough accepted students decide to go elsewhere. Most colleges rank their waitlists. You can ask where you sit on the list, your chances of being accepted, and when.

- DEFERRED: This is the other limbo. You're not in, out, or on the waitlist. It's not common, but sometimes admissions committees defer a decision because they want more information, like more of your senior year grades, or to clarify something that came up when assessing your application.

Early Decision applications can be deferred to the regular admission pool, which means your application will be reviewed with the regular pool and you may be asked for additional information. A deferral also releases you from the commitment to attend, if accepted in the spring.

The Final Steps for Regular Admissions

With acceptances in hand, it's time to turn the tables back again. Make the colleges and universities compete for your enrollment. The extra effort you will have put into the process pays off here.

These are the final steps:

- Cross declines off your list; they're done.
- Set waitlists aside, for now.
- Review your big-picture thoughts to help dial in on what matters the most.
- Complete a final evaluation of each college that now includes the actual cost.
- If you have to negotiate a financial aid package, do it now— respectfully and with low expectations.
- Rank your list from top to bottom, using tiebreakers if everything else is equal.

- If you're on a waitlist, review your evaluation of this college/ university, compare it to the others on your list, and decide if it's worth the wait. If not, cross it off.

- If a waitlist school is worth the extra time and effort, ask about the chances for acceptance, potential financial aid, and when you're likely to know. This information should be balanced with the notification deadlines for colleges that accept you.

Be deliberate. Don't rush. Only the deadline matters when informing a college that you want to enroll.

The Final Steps for Early Decision

Because of the commitment to attend, an Early Decision application is the final decision on where you want to go, if accepted. The last steps for an Early Decision application are similar, but a little different than deciding on a college in the regular cycle.

Here are the final steps:

- Review your Big Picture thoughts.

- Complete a final evaluation for the colleges on your Top Shelf, *including* a specific plan for a foundational experience at each one.

- Determine the estimated cost *with a buffer* in case the financial aid package is less than expected.

- Rank your list from top to bottom, using tiebreakers if everything else is equal.

- Visit the college/university *before* you apply to make sure it's worthy of such a major commitment. If your rankings are close, visit the top two or three to confirm your evaluations.

- *Only apply early to a clear winner.* Avoid the commitment to attend if two or three are really close.

- *Be sure to have a strong reason for applying early.* One that can stand up over time, instead of a desire to be done with it.
- *Do not assume you'll be accepted.* That means you should still prepare to apply to other colleges. Chip away at this preparation to avoid having to rush on future applications.

It's okay to *accelerate the process* when deciding on early decision, just don't jump the process or fall victim to decision fatigue.

Back to the regular admissions cycle.

A Key Decision Point

If there is a large gap in total cost between two or three colleges, you might have trouble ranking acceptances. Go with the lower-cost option, if everything else is equal.

Some students are vexed by differences in cost. If that happens, pull affordability from your evaluations, which allows you to rank the foundational experience on an apples-to-apples basis. Then, compare the experience for each college to the total cost.

If a college costs significantly more, but anchors the best experience:

- Is the additional cost worth the greater benefit of this experience?
- Is there any element/activity you missed on the lower-cost experience that could legitimately close the gap on the higher cost option?
- If not, would the cost savings be worth a lesser experience?

This is a straight cost/benefit comparison, and you will probably need advice from others.

The Decision is Clear

Many students will find a college/university emerges as the clear winner. If that happens, you have a decision! Exhale and celebrate.

Splitting Hairs

Even after accounting for tiebreakers, some students can still be splitting hairs on two or three opportunities. First, be grateful for a nice problem. Then, walk away from the decision for a day or two, even a week, if necessary. Afterward, take a fresh look at these colleges/universities.

If a winner becomes clear, you're done. You have a decision! Exhale and celebrate.

If you're still stuck after such an informed process, there's only one way to resolve it. Go with your heart.

I bet you didn't see that coming. And now, you have a decision! Exhale and celebrate.

No matter how your winner emerges, be proud of the professional-caliber decision you have made.

Chapter 36

FINAL THOUGHTS

This Is Your Time

"I wish it need not have happened in my time," said Frodo.
"So do I," said Gandalf, "and so do all who live to see
such times. But that is not for them to decide.
All we have to decide is what to do
with the time that is given us."[1]

J. R. R. Tolkien, Lord of the Rings, Book One,
The Fellowship of the Ring

You will never regret the advantage gained from a proper search and foundational life experience in your college years. The education you receive, mental and transferable skills you develop, and the fundamentals you learn for making decisions will have lasting value for the rest of your life.

Kryptonite

There's only one bit of advice left to cover. It's very important, but I waited until the end for two reasons:

1. Any student who has read this all the way through will have the discipline to stick with the advice; and

2. I didn't want to do the cranky-old-man thing right out of the gate.

---

1   J. R. R. Tolkien, *Lord of the Rings, Book One, The Fellowship of the Ring* (Great Britain: HarperCollins Publisher, 2004), 51.

We covered the human superpower—our shared ability to think and learn—and that our only option is to develop these skills. This takes time, but distractions are kryptonite.

For your generation, that means phones, tablets, laptops, video games, movies, television, etc. Technology will play a major role throughout your search and during your time in college, but *as a tool, not a distraction*. You will need to carve out time to focus with a deep commitment during the moments that matter. Yes, that means disconnecting from social media.

And please ignore the multitasking fantasy. That just splits up your time and leaves you with shallower commitments across many moments.

When Eagles Launch

You're already on a path to excelling in life. Always remember: when eagles launch, they take a leap of faith every time. You can put the same level of faith in your best effort. Play hard. Play the game the right way. Then, whatever happens will happen, and you can deal with it then.

This is *your* time, so make it count! Try, fail, reflect, correct.

APPENDIX

Resources Cited and Templates for Evaluation, Sorting, and Planning

This Appendix contains follow-up material to assist your search and decision.

Below are two versions of the evaluation template. The first version includes notes for clarification along with questions to consider for some of the criteria. Remember, not all of the questions necessarily apply to you. Use your judgment on these.

The second version of the evaluation template is a clean copy without notes or questions, which is also downloadable at *wheneagleslaunch.com*. You can use this for evaluations, clicking "save as" to create a new evaluation.

After these evaluation templates, you'll find two more. The first is the template for sorting your college list by shelves and balancing your chances for admissions—*Probables*, *Reasonables*, and *Long Shots*. The second is the planning template for a foundational life experience. These are also available at *wheneagleslaunch.com*.

Finally, there is a list of the resources cited for financial aid, sourcing potential college/universities, and advice on applications. All of the data points you need to fill out your evaluations can be found in the sources listed here.

I hope all of these are helpful.

WHEN EAGLES LAUNCH - COLLEGE/UNIVERSITY EVALUATION TEMPLATE
(With Notes)

Name of Institution:

_____

SIZE, LOCATION, AND SETTING: _____
(5, 4, 3, 2, or 1)

Enrollment: _____

Region: _____
(e.g., Midwest, West, etc.)

Campus Setting: _____
(Urban, Rural, Suburban)

Comments:

Consider the positives, negatives, and trade-offs in relation to your needs.

_____

AFFORDABILITY: _____
(5, 4, 3, 2, or 1)

Full Cost Per Year: $_____
(Includes tuition, room, board, fees, etc.)

Financial Aid Estimate: $_____
(Use financial calculators)

Official Financial Aid Offer: $_____

Net Price Per Year: $_____
(Full Cost minus Financial Aid)

Estimated Four-Year Cost: $_____
(Net Price over four years with % increases included for each year. You can make it five years for a more conservative estimate.)

Average Student Loan Debt: $_____

Comments:

Other Considerations

- *Are work/study options available?*

- *Are merit scholarships awarded? Do you have a chance to qualify?*

ACADEMIC FIT: _____
(5, 4, 3, 2, or 1)

Average SAT/ACT Scores: ___/___
(75%/25%)

Average GPA: _____

Ave. High School Class Rank - Top 10%: _____%

- Top 25%: _____%

Average Class Size: _____

Student to Faculty Ratio: _____

Graduation Rate - Four-year: _____%

- Six-year: _____%

Retention Rate: _____%
(% of students returning after first year)

Your List of Possible Majors: 1)_____

(At least three) 2)_____

3)_____

4)_____

5)_____

Comments:

Other Considerations:

Quality of teaching and learning environment:

- *Is there a mix of learning options through the traditional classroom, technology, and experiential/hands-on projects?*

- *Do professors teach all classes? If not, how much do they rely on graduate teaching assistants?*

- *Does high-course demand push students to take online courses?*

Graduation requirements and elective options:

- *Would the general education requirements for graduation (core curriculum) expose you to important areas beyond a major?*

- *How many elective courses (beyond requirements) could you take and which ones interest you?*

- *Is there an introductory course/program to help with the transition to college level work?*

- *Can you identify courses/programs that would advance important transferable skills?*

- *Do any special programs/unique features interest you?*

- *Are there study abroad options that interest you? Could any delay graduation?*

Academic advising and other support services:

- *Would the advice you need be available?*

- *How often can you meet with your advisor?*

- *Is general academic support or help with specific classes readily available?*

- *Is academic advice linked with career advice?*

CAREER SERVICES: _____
(5, 4, 3, 2, or 1)

Comments:

Considerations:

- *When can students start working with career counselors?*
- *What is the job placement record beyond finance, law, medicine, and consulting?*
- *How will the office help you find internships?*
- *Does the office offer personal assessments to identify interests and strengths/weaknesses for professions?*
- *How much of the office's resources are available after graduation?*
- *How strong is the alumni network? How willing are alumni to help students?*

STUDENT SERVICES AND ACTIVITIES: _____
(5, 4, 3, 2, or 1)

Comments:

Considerations:

- *Is there a strong orientation program to help students transition to college life?*
- *Are student support services, like health and wellness, readily available?*
- *Are there opportunities for healthy social interactions? Do a lot of students go home on weekends?*
- *What percentage of students live off campus?*
- *Is there a range of activities? Which ones would advance your habits of mind and transferable skills?*

- *Does the campus layout facilitate a balance between classes and student activities?*

- *Are you comfortable with campus safety measures?*

TIEBREAKERS: _____
(5, 4, 3, 2, or 1)

Comments:

Considerations:
- *Quality of housing, campus beauty, facilities, amenities, food, etc.*

OVERALL RATING: _____
(Top Shelf, Middle Shelf, or Bottom Shelf)

CHANCES FOR ADMISSIONS: _____
(Probable, Reasonable, or Long Shot)

Summary Comments:

Summarize your evaluation—noting the pros and cons—and explain your ratings (e.g., Top Shelf, Reasonable). There is not a final average for your ratings (e.g., 4.7, 3.9, 2.8) because you might consider one or two criteria to be more important than others. Feel free to average them if you want or to develop a weighted average that emphasizes certain criteria more than others. If you need to create additional criteria, add them before the Tiebreakers Rating.

WHEN EAGLES LAUNCH - COLLEGE/UNIVERSITY EVALUATION TEMPLATE

(Without Notes)

Name of Institution:

SIZE, LOCATION, AND SETTING: _____

    Enrollment: _____

    Region: _____

    Campus Setting: _____

<u>**Comments:**</u>

AFFORDABILITY: _____

    Full Cost Per Year: $_____

    Financial Aid Estimate: $_____

    Official Financial Aid Offer: $_____

    Net Price Per Year: $_____

    Estimated Four-Year Cost: $_____

    Average Student Loan Debt: $_____

Comments:

_____

ACADEMIC FIT: _____

    Average SAT/ACT Scores: ___/___

    Average GPA: _____

    Ave. High School Class Rank - Top 10%:   _____%

                                          - Top 25%:   _____%

    Average Class Size: _____

    Student to Faculty Ratio: _____

    Graduation Rate - Four-year: _____%

                                - Six-year: _____%

    Retention Rate: _____

    Your List of Possible Majors: 1)_____

                                          2)_____

                                          3)_____

                                          4)_____

                                          5)_____

Comments:

CAREER SERVICES: _____

Comments:

STUDENT SERVICES AND ACTIVITIES: _____

Comments:

TIEBREAKERS: _____

Comments:

OVERALL RATING: _____

CHANCES FOR ADMISSIONS: _____

<u>**Summary Comments:**</u>

WHEN EAGLES LAUNCH - SORTING BY SHELVES

	<u>Probables</u>	<u>Reasonables</u>	<u>Long Shots</u> *(Optional)*
Top Shelf	- _____	- _____	- _____
	- _____	- _____	- _____
	- _____	- _____	- _____

Middle Shelf	- _____	- _____	- _____
	- _____	- _____	- _____
	- _____	- _____	- _____

Bottom Shelf   *(A list of the other colleges/universities you evaluated.)*

WHEN EAGLES LAUNCH - PLANNING TEMPLATE FOR A FOUNDATIONAL LIFE EXPERIENCE

Time Period	Activities	Transferable Skills Acquired	Reasons
STAGE 1 Exploration:			
Time Before College			
First Academic Year			
Summer			
Second Academic Year			
Summer			
STAGE 2 Professional Pursuit:			
Third Academic Year			
Summer			
Fourth Academic Year			
Time After College			

This is a representation of what your template should look like. Obviously, the boxes will need to be bigger when you fill them out. Feel free to alter the structure *within* either stage, depending on what a college offers. If summer classes are necessary, add them. Remember to develop a flexible plan that should evolve as you gather advice throughout college. The downloadable version at *wheneagleslaunch.com* has expandable boxes.

LIST OF RESOURCES CITED

Financial Aid (Chapter 27)

- The Pay for College tab includes a link to Financial Aid 101 on The College Board's Big Future website (*www.bigfuture. collegeboard.org*).

- The *U.S. News* website has useful information, including College Financial Aid 101, which can be found in the Paying For College section (*https://www.usnews.com/education/ best-colleges/paying-for-college/financial-aid-101*).

- Lynn O'Shaughnessy's book, *The College Solution*, helps students find the right school at the right price.[1]

- FinAid (*www.finaid.org*).

- Sallie Mae (*www.salliemae.com)* has information on student loans and financial aid.

Financial Aid Applications (Chapter 27)

- FAFSA® (*http://fafsa.ed.gov*): Free Application for Federal Student Aid (FAFSA®) is the federal form for financial aid used by public colleges and universities. You can get an estimate on your *expected family contribution* (EFC) at *https:// studentaid.ed.gov/sa/fafsa/estimate.*

- The CSS Profile™ (*https://cssprofile.collegeboard.org*) is required by many private institutions to determine eligibility for aid.

Financial Aid Calculators (Chapter 27)

- Calculators are available on most college and university websites.

- The Big Future and FinAid sites (see above) have them.

---

[1]   Lynn O'Shaughnessy, *The College Solution* (Upper Saddle River, New Jersey: Pearson Education, Inc., 2012).

- Lynn O'Shaughnessy has useful advice on calculators at *http://www.thecollegesolution.com/ why-you-must-use-college-net-price-calculators/*.

Initial Screening of Possible Colleges/Universities (Chapter 32)

Websites:

- College Navigator (*http://nces.ed.gov/collegenavigator/*)
- The College Board's Big Future website (*https://bigfuture. collegeboard.org*)
- Niche (*https://www.niche.com*)

Online College Guides:

- *Peterson's* (*www.petersons.com*)
- *The Princeton Review* (*www.princetonreview.com*)
- *U.S. News & World Report* (*www.usnews.com/best-colleges*)

Printed Guidebooks:

- *Barron's Profiles of American Colleges*
- *Fiske Guide to Colleges*
- *The Ultimate Guide to America's Best Colleges*

Submitting Applications (Chapter 34)

- The *Applying 101* section of The College Board's Big Future website *https://bigfuture.collegeboard.org/get-in/applying.*
- *Admission Matters*—Part 3: Tackling Your Applications.[2]

Application Essays

- The Essays section of The College Board's Big Future website (*https://bigfuture.collegeboard.org/get-in/essays*)
- *Admission Matters* (See above)

---

2   Sally P. Springer, Jon Reider, and Joyce Vining Morgan, *Admission Matters* (San Francisco: Jossey-Bass, 2017).

ACKNOWLEDGMENTS

Writing a book is a solo effort. At least, that's what I thought when starting this project, which turned out to be three books. The first two are different versions of this one, and they'll never see the light of day. Still, they were an important part of the learning process.

Yes, I had to try, fail, reflect, correct—all the way through.

But back to the solo effort, which evolved into a team effort. Over time, a formal group of professionals, along with an informal group of volunteer readers and friends had formed. Without their help, encouragement, and terrific insights along the way, I would never have made it to the finish line.

First, I have to thank Kelley, my wife of thirty-plus years. Without her incredible grace, patience, love, and support throughout the entire process, what you've just read would not exist. Looking back, I can't imagine how difficult it was to deal with a husband who suddenly comes down with a really bad case of book brain. And I wasn't exactly a prize before that, either.

I also must thank my children, Jake and Emily, who first lived through much of the content in this book, and then offered unyielding encouragement and valuable advice throughout the process.

At different stages, my editors Jill Welch, Heather May, and Erin Seaward-Hiatt each did a fantastic job moving the project along. Thank you for your professionalism, quality work, and dealing with a rookie writer who asked a lot of dumb questions. Any errors are mine. Erin, thank you for a great cover design, too.

Katie Mullaly of Surrogate Press® was invaluable as well, guiding me through the process and taking the written manuscript through the important steps to becoming an actual book.

Finally, Nancy Sayles—a tenacious publicist—has been invaluable in helping to build awareness of the book and guiding me through the process.

I stress the importance of feedback throughout the book, and when writing one, it's critical. What makes so much sense in a writer's mind almost always turns out to be scrambled eggs in the early drafts. Then, when it seems to be right on paper, a lot of it makes sense only to the author and a few others, not a broad audience. This is the insanity of writing, which is actually a very long, challenging process of rewriting—think of shoveling snow endlessly in a blizzard.

That's why I am so grateful to my readers. The following people read chapters or entire drafts of the book at different stages of its development: Christie Delbridge, Bob Mackey, Lisa Trieman, Gerry Trieman, Colter Pruyn, Rich Alderete, Peter Rescigno, Terry "Sir Terrence" Goodman, Phil Rubin, Alana Urie, Cindy Skelton, Kim Keene, Ray Grass, Eric Savage, Jonathan Brand, Marnie Keator, Gerrit Keator, Andrew Acuna, James Thompson, Bekah Keator, Marina Keator, Peter Erickson, Emily Battaglia, and Brad Kliber.

You each offered great insights, encouragement, and feedback that, when necessary, was blunt, bracing, and to the point, which I loved. You all contributed to the content or the way in which it is written, and I will always be grateful for your time and effort.

There is one reader who deserves special recognition. Max Larson read two versions of the book. He was my first reader during the summer between his junior and senior years of high school. He slogged through what was a very rough draft at a time when I was looking for an excuse to pull the plug. It was Max's enthusiasm for that material and his feedback that kept me going. Max then read an improved version before his first year of college, and his greater enthusiasm for the progress made to that point was critical in helping me see it through. Max, thank you! (And for potential employers: you're crazy if you don't hire him.)

Beyond readers, there is a large group of people who have helped the project through their encouragement, insights, support, or conversations in which I could test ideas. So a heartfelt thank you to Steve Frank, Lynn Regester, Anne Frank, Michael McGlauflin, Craig McCarthy, John Adams, Sage Mora, Rich Gavril, Jim Martz, Floyd Inman, Kim Mackey, Roseanne Power, Karen Scheible, Chance Cook, Connie Iglesias Martin, John Adams, Steve Wilson, Tristian Pierson, Craig Struthers, Chris Lampe, Khaki Howe, Amy Silverston, Steve Mullins, Eugene McCarthy, Linda McCullough Moore, Stan and Kim Sadowski, Jonathan Howe, Ann O'Keefe, Cheryl Tupper, Lesley Roberts, Doreen Gross, Allen Mast, David Rotman, John Crosson, Roy O'Bannon, Diane Jacobsen, Page Juliano, Bill Ligety, Abbi Martz, Charly Ligety, Valen Lindner, Jamison Frost, Susan and Jim Noyes, Joyce Reed, Mike Bryan, and last but far from least, the now former Emily Witte.

I also need to thank the entire DVGS crew—winter and summer—for creating such a tremendous work environment. It's rare that a group of people with such diverse ages and backgrounds can have so much fun working as hard as we do. Being able to look forward to work—even when we're going get slammed—played a critical part in seeing this project through.

Finally, you probably noticed I have great respect for teachers, coaches, and parents who take the time to do it right. I was very fortunate to benefit from all three, and will always be grateful for their time and extra effort, especially my parents.

ABOUT THE AUTHOR

A former teacher and coach, William Keator spent seventeen years at the Arthur Vining Davis Foundations, where he directed their national Higher Education and Secondary Education programs. The Higher Education program supported a range of colleges and universities across the country, while the Secondary Education program awarded grants to new and innovative programs for the professional development of high school teachers.

Before joining the Foundations, William served as the first Program Officer for the Jacksonville Jaguars Foundation, the philanthropic arm of the then newly-established National Football League (NFL) franchise. He assisted in the development of the foundation's community-based grant program, and directed several award-winning programs serving disadvantaged youth in greater Jacksonville, Florida.

William came to the Jaguars Foundation in 1995 after working in New York for the NFL's Player Programs department, which provided continuing education, financial education, and career internships for active NFL players. This included helping develop the *NFL Rookie Symposium*, which became a signature program in player management for over twenty years.

Prior to joining the NFL, William earned a Master's Degree from the Harvard University Graduate School of Education in 1993.

Made in the USA
Middletown, DE
20 January 2022

59211963R00161